Lucy Huskinson is Lecturer in the School of Theology and Religious Studies at Bangor University. She is the author of *Nietzsche and Jung: The Whole Self in the Union of Opposites* and editor and contributor to *Dreaming the Myth Onwards: New Directions in Jungian Therapy and Thought*, both published by Routledge.

An Introduction to

Nietzsche

Lucy Huskinson

 HENDRICKSON
PUBLISHERS

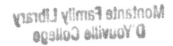

First published jointly in Great Britain in 2009

as *The SPCK Introduction to Nietzsche* by
Society for Promoting Christian Knowledge
36 Causton Street
London SW1P 4ST

and in the USA as *An Introduction to Nietzsche* by
Hendrickson Publishers Marketing, LLC
P.O. Box 3473
Peabody, Massachusetts 01961-3473

British Library Cataloguing-in-Publication Data
A catalogue record for this book is available from the British Library

SPCK ISBN 978–0–281–06042–9
Hendrickson Publishers ISBN 978–1–59856–470–9

1 3 5 7 9 10 8 6 4 2

Typeset by Graphicraft Limited, Hong Kong
Printed in Great Britain by Ashford Colour Press

Produced on paper from sustainable forests

For
Eleanor and Catrin
through whom I joyfully overcome my compulsion
for Nietzschean free-spiritedness

Contents

Acknowledgements

I wish to thank Rebecca Mulhearn at SPCK for her support throughout the various stages of the book's production. My thanks also go to Lauren Chiosso and Rima Devereaux, and to Neil Whyte for his sharp eye and impressive editorial skill. I am grateful to Christopher Jones and Natalie Haystead for the photograph on the book's cover, which depicts Natalie – an undergraduate student of mine – on the steps leading to the 'Private/Preifat' door of Bangor Cathedral. It is my hope that Nietzschean thought will one day be welcomed inside.

My greatest thanks and appreciation are due to the following people, who have made invaluable contributions to the realization of this book. To Carina, Bali and Catrin for creating time and extending space; to David for elucidation and direction; and to Eryl for making me laugh to the grounds of my being at the most inopportune moments.

Abbreviations

Nietzsche's works are abbreviated as follows. Numeric references in the text are to *section* numbers.

AC   *The Anti-Christ: Curse on Christianity* (1888), translated by R. J. Hollingdale, Harmondsworth: Penguin, 1990.

BGE   *Beyond Good and Evil: Prelude to a Philosophy of the Future* (1886), translated by R. J. Hollingdale, Harmondsworth: Penguin, 1990.

BT   *The Birth of Tragedy out of the Spirit of Music* (1872), edited by Michael Tanner, translated by Shaun Whiteside, Harmondsworth: Penguin, 1993.

D   *Daybreak: Thoughts on the Prejudices of Morality* (1881), edited by Maudmarie Clark and Brian Leiter, translated by R. J. Hollingdale, Cambridge: Cambridge University Press, 1997.

EH   *Ecce Homo: How One Becomes What One Is* (1888), translated by R. J. Hollingdale, Harmondsworth: Penguin, 1990.

GM (I–IV) *On the Genealogy of Morals: A Polemic* (1887), translated by Walter Kaufmann, New York: Random House, 1968.

GS   *The Gay Science* (1882), translated by Walter Kaufmann, New York: Vintage, 1974.

HAH   *Human, All Too Human: A Book For Free Spirits* (1878), translated by R. J. Hollingdale, Cambridge: Cambridge University Press, 1996.

PTAG   *Philosophy in the Tragic Age of the Greeks* (1873; unpublished by Nietzsche), translated by M. Cowan, Chicago: Regnery, 1962.

TI   *Twilight of the Idols, or How to Philosophize with a Hammer* (1888), translated by R. J. Hollingdale, Harmondsworth: Penguin, 1990.

TSZ (I–IV)   *Thus Spoke Zarathustra: A Book for Everyone and No One* (1883–5), translated by R. J. Hollingdale, Harmondsworth: Penguin, 1961.

UM (I–IV)   *Untimely Meditations* (1873–6), translated by R. J. Hollingdale, Cambridge: Cambridge University Press, 1983.

WP   *The Will to Power*, edited by Walter Kaufmann, translated by Walter Kaufmann and R. J. Hollingdale, New York: Vintage, 1967. This edition follows the 1911 German edition.

WS   *The Wanderer and His Shadow* (*HAH* III, 1880), translated by R. J. Hollingdale, Cambridge: Cambridge University Press, 1996.

Date chart

1844	Friedrich Wilhelm Nietzsche was born in Röcken, in the Prussian province of Saxony, on 15 October.
1846	Birth of sister Elisabeth.
1849	Birth of brother Joseph. Death of his father Karl Ludwig (a Lutheran minister) due to 'softening of the brain' following a fall.
1850	Death of brother; family moves to Naumburg to live with father's mother and her sisters.
1858–64	Attends renowned school at Pforta, and excels in classics and religious studies.
1861	Nietzsche confirmed at Easter.
1864	Enrols at Bonn University to read theology and classical philology.
1865	Transfers from Bonn to Leipzig University to follow his classics professor, where he drops theology and continues classical philology. Discovers Schopenhauer's *The World as Will and Representation*. Refuses to take communion on Easter Sunday.
1867–8	Military service in Naumburg, where he suffers chest wound.
1868	Returns to Leipzig, where he meets Richard Wagner for the first time.
1869	Appointed Professor of Classical Philology at Basel University. Awarded doctorate without examination. Renounces Prussian citizenship and fails in his application for Swiss citizenship (and is stateless for rest of his life).
1870	Serves as volunteer hospital attendant in Franco–Prussian War. Witnesses traumatic effects of battle, and contracts diphtheria and dysentery.
1872	Publishes *The Birth of Tragedy* to mixed reviews.

1873–6	Publishes *Untimely Meditations*.
1876	Breaks with Wagner after attending first Bayreuth Festival. Granted full year of sick leave from the University due to further illness.
1878–9	Publishes *Human, All Too Human*, which confirms break with Wagner.
1879	Retires from Basel University due to ill health. Publishes *Assorted Opinions and Maxims* (supplement to *HAH*).
1880–9	Lives nomadic life living and travelling mostly in France, Italy and Switzerland.
1880	Publishes *Wanderer and His Shadow* (*HAH* III).
1881	Publishes *Daybreak*.
1882	Publishes *The Gay Science*. Meets and becomes infatuated with Lou Andreas-Salomé, who spurns his marriage proposals.
1883–5	Publishes *Thus Spoke Zarathustra*.
1886	Publishes *Beyond Good and Evil*.
1887	Publishes *On the Genealogy of Morals*.
1888	Begins to receive public recognition (with the lectures on his work given by Georg Brandes in Copenhagen). Nietzsche's final active year, in which he completes *The Wagner Case: Twilight of the Idols* (1889); *The Anti-Christ* (1895); *Ecce Homo* (1908); *Nietzsche contra Wagner* (1895); and *Dionysus Dithyrambs* (1892).
1889	Collapses on a street in Turin (3 January) after witnessing the beating of a horse. Nietzsche suffers a supposed mental breakdown and paralysis of body and mind. Committed to an asylum in Jena.
1890	Discharged into the care of his mother in Naumburg.
1894	His sister Elisabeth founds Nietzsche Archives (in Naumburg, moving it to Weimar in 1896).
1897	Mother dies; Elisabeth moves Nietzsche to Weimar.
1900	Nietzsche dies in Weimar on 25 August.

Introduction

Readers may be astonished to find the inclusion of Friedrich Nietzsche in this introductory series to Christian thinkers. After all, Nietzsche not only pronounced the 'death of God' and the need to go 'beyond good and evil', but he also portrayed Christians as 'weak degenerates' and extolled the virtues of the Antichrist! At face value Nietzsche's ideas appear blasphemous and totally unconstructive for Christians. However, it is this kind of superficial impression of Nietzsche that this introductory work seeks to dispel, and in the process it will seek to reveal his relevance for Christians today.

Nietzsche is one of the most iconic thinkers of our time, whose thought shaped modern Western thought; and he is widely revered as a pioneer of postmodernism. And yet he is also one of the most abused and misunderstood. All too often he is dismissed as a mad, ranting atheist with eccentric and incredible ideas. Without a doubt there are grounds for such a caricature. He was certainly an eccentric personality, and he did launch a ferocious assault on Christianity. Furthermore, his cryptic writing style, which is steeped in metaphor and contradiction, positively encourages misunderstanding. Yet to dismiss him on this basis is to pass over a rich and potent narrative that is extremely relevant to Christians today, and indeed to anybody concerned with a meaningful life.

This book does not pretend that Nietzsche's thought can be aligned with Christianity, and neither does it adopt clever tricks of interpretation to portray Nietzsche as a closet Christian. Indeed, the sole fact that Nietzsche explicitly rejects Christ makes any such attempt futile and fundamentally flawed. What this book does attempt to do, however, is to outline Nietzsche's search for, and explanation of, authentic divinity, through his destruction of what he deems to be the dehumanizing and corrupt values of Christianity, and his subsequent creation of a 'new' faith grounded in the affirmation of life. It is important to mention here that in no way did Nietzsche seek to establish a new religion or to resurrect a paganism of the past. Indeed, just a few months before his mental breakdown, Nietzsche writes in his brief autobiography, *Ecce Homo* (which is more of a survey of his published works over the previous 16 years than about his personal life):

> [T]here is nothing in me of a founder of religion – religions are affairs of the rabble . . . I do not *want* 'believers' . . . I have a terrible fear that I will one day be pronounced *holy*.

Nietzsche's quest is for what he calls 'the revaluation of values', and this, as will be shown, is not a new set or system of values, but a new way of valuing, living and relating to the world.

In the hope of encouraging greater dialogue between Nietzsche and Christian thought, the following pages aim to clarify obscure notions in Nietzsche's thought and to dispel common misperceptions about them.

Nietzsche is associated with many slogans and catchphrases that, when viewed out of their context, contribute to Nietzsche's distorted image and unsavoury caricature. Thus, 'will to power', 'God is dead', 'the superman', 'master morality', 'beyond good and evil' and 'philosophizing with a hammer' may themselves suggest a destructive and egocentric viewpoint and the advocacy of domination and oppression of the weak through brute force. But when viewed within the context of Nietzsche's 'religious' critique, we find this is far from the case. Thus, as we shall see in the course of our discussion, according to Nietzsche, the superman (*Übermensch* or 'overhuman') exercises his or her will to power as an act of spiritual strength over him or herself. Furthermore, the death of God leads not to nihilism and anarchy but to a loss that demands affirmation, and through this affirmation we find our lives enriched with greater closeness to being, and the realization of a proper divinity. We shall see that the existence of God is not at stake for Nietzsche. He is concerned, rather, with the relinquishing of defunct and corrupt values and the creation of new ones that are more pertinent to life, in which divinity is experienced afresh and alive.

There are several reasons why Nietzsche's work is so readily misunderstood. His writing style, which has already been mentioned, is often intentionally obscure, dense and misleading in order to present a variety of different perspectives (which, as we shall see, is integral to his philosophical position and faith in the affirmation of life). Nietzsche does not want to commit his ideas to one meaning or interpretation, and seeks to avoid systematization of thought. To this end he often writes in aphorisms (short passages, from one or two lines to a few pages, as we see especially in *HAH*, *D* and *BGE*), the content of which contradicts and distorts as much as it enlightens. For example, we can even find such ambiguity and apparent inconsistency in his views on Christianity and religious people generally. On the one hand, he regards the Christian as 'the domestic animal, the herd animal, the sick animal man', 'physiologically retarded, weak' (*AC* 3) and he complains that 'I have need of washing my hands after contact with religious people (*EH*, 'Why I am a destiny' 1). Yet on the other hand, Nietzsche reveres the nobility and strength of the Christian to the extent that he celebrates the hands that soiled his own. Christianity has:

> *chiselled out* perhaps the most refined figures in human society that have ever yet existed: the figures of the higher and highest Catholic priesthood, especially when they have descended from a noble race and brought with them an inborn grace of gesture, the eye of command, and beautiful hands and feet.   (*D* 60)

Similarly, 'Who could possibly feel an aversion for pious people strong in their faith? To the contrary, do we not regard them with a silent respect and take pleasure in them . . . ?' (*D* 56).

Nietzsche's work is a tangled yet eloquent mix of self-contradiction. Indeed, one stand-alone aphorism of Nietzsche's is very pertinent if we apply his words to his own writings: 'This thinker needs no one to refute him: he does that for himself'

(*WS* 249). Furthermore, the many contrasting perspectives of Nietzsche's thought mean there are as many 'Nietzsches' to interpret. Indeed, the Nietzschean scholar Steven E. Ascheim shows how we can scavenge among Nietzsche's texts to find intellectual support for almost any ideological position, including anarchist, expressionist, feminist, misogynist, futurist, nationalist, Nazi, sexual-libertarian, socialist, *völkisch*, Zionist, Catholic, Protestant, deconstructionist, postmodernist, vegetarian, and so on.

This book does not profess yet another interpretation of Nietzsche as the 'correct' one, and neither does it merely survey the many 'Nietzsches' that manifest themselves in Nietzschean scholarship. Rather, it will argue that Nietzsche's meaning is found in the creative tension between multiple interpretations, and that the key to understanding him is through your own subjective response to his writings. This is not to say, however, that Nietzsche cannot be misunderstood or that any interpretation or perspective is as appropriate as the next. It is precisely this democratic and nihilistic attitude Nietzsche wishes to overcome. Indeed, the final sentence of his final book, *EH*, begins with the troubled words, '*Have I been understood?*'

Perhaps the most notorious misunderstanding and misappropriation of Nietzsche's work – which has left an indelible stain on Nietzsche's reputation – is by the German National Socialist party. The Nazi party bastardized Nietzschean thought according to its own power-hungry ends, and in the process turned the spiritual *Übermenschen* into the dominant 'master race' of the Third Reich. The fact that Nietzsche vigorously opposed German nationalism, mocked the idea of a Teutonic master race, and both despised anti-Semitism in all its forms and revered the Jewish nation (at least prior to its Exile) is often eclipsed by the perverted version of Nietzsche presented to the world by his Fascist younger sister, Elisabeth. Elisabeth enjoyed strong connections with the Nazi party, having married the ferociously anti-Semitic Bernhard Förster (with whom she sought to establish a 'pure' Aryan republic in

Paraguay called *Nueva Germania* or 'New Germany') and befriended Hitler himself (who attended her funeral in 1935). Nietzsche outwardly renounced his sister's views to the extent that he was compelled to break personal ties with her.[1] After Nietzsche's death, Elisabeth seized upon his extensive archive of unpublished writings and notes (referred to as the *Nachlass*) and appointed herself sole executor of his literary estate (for which she received financial support and publicity from the Nazi party). At this time she reconstructed Nietzsche as the mythical intellectual forerunner of National Socialism. To this end she hastily yet heavily doctored his notes, and published them in his name as *The Will to Power* – a book Elisabeth claimed best reflected her brother's philosophical project.

This introduction to Nietzsche's religious thought seeks to rescue his faith from the murky misunderstandings that surround his confusing work, and it attempts to do so in four parts. Roughly speaking these parts form a sequence of themes, but they can also be read as self-contained chapters. The first chapter outlines Nietzsche's critique of – or attack on – Christianity; the second describes the implications of his critique through his important idea of the death of God; the third explores Nietzsche's vision of a new faith in the overcoming of Christianity; and the fourth chapter explains how Nietzsche's thought is directly relevant to Christians today. This final chapter offers a reading of Nietzsche that may appear controversial, especially to the reader who remains committed to the idea that Nietzsche's work is completely hostile to and unconstructive for Christian thought. It contends that Nietzsche's target audience is Christian, and that his writings intend to provoke Christians with a timely wake-up call. In particular, it highlights those aspects of Nietzsche's critique of Christianity that expose problems within Christian discipleship, such as the common inability among Christians to comprehend the meaning of faith, and to realize how excruciatingly difficult and 'serious' it is both to *live* an authentically Christian life and to facilitate the life-enhancing force of Christianity.

Friedrich Nietzsche, the man

For Nietzsche, ideas cannot be considered in isolation from their authors. 'Every great philosophy', he writes, 'has hitherto been a confession on the part of its author and a kind of involuntary and unconscious memoir' (*BGE* 6). Furthermore, 'our most sacred convictions' are, he says, simply 'the judgements of our muscles'. In this respect, philosophy, psychology and physiology are inextricably linked. And Nietzsche's own writings are, he claims, written with his whole body. Therefore to learn about Friedrich Nietzsche, the man, Nietzsche would have us examine his writings. Indeed, some scholars, such as the analytical psychologist C. G. Jung, have attempted to psychoanalyse his texts to expose the personality behind them. However, just as there are many perspectives within Nietzsche's writings, there seem to be several masks that obscure the personality of the author. Certainly, it is easier to find an idealization of Nietzsche the person, rather than a realistic portrayal of who he actually was. For instance, while Nietzsche wrote about 'the great health', 'nobility', and 'affirmation', Nietzsche himself was a rather pathetic man, whose life was plagued by continual ill health, depression and loneliness. Indeed, in his 1888 preface to *HAH*, he concedes that he composed his notion of the 'free spirits' (which we will examine in Chapter 3) in order to compensate for the friends he lacked. He tells us he would laugh and chatter to his phantom companions, who would subsequently keep him in 'good spirits'. Some scholars (including C. G. Jung, Georges Bataille and René Girard) have argued that in addition to Nietzsche's psychological or physiological disposition, it was the very content of his ideas that led to his mental and physical demise.

Friedrich Nietzsche was born in Röcken (near Leipzig), in the Prussian province of Saxony, on 15 October 1844. This date coincided with the 49th birthday of the Prussian King, Friedrich Wilhelm IV, after whom Nietzsche was named. Nietzsche was born into a long line of Lutheran ministers.[2] His paternal grandfather, Friedrich August Ludwig Nietzsche, was a distinguished Protestant scholar who wrote several books, one of which, *Gamaliel* (1796), somewhat ironically earned a honorary doctorate for its excellent defence of Christianity and its argument for Christianity's 'everlasting survival'. Nietzsche's father (also a Lutheran pastor) died of a brain ailment when Nietzsche was four years old, an event that, together with the death of his youngest brother six months later, caused the young 'Fritz' immense distress (which he would later recall in his writing) and resulted in his having to spend his childhood in the company of a household of women: his mother, his sister Elisabeth and two maiden aunts.

Nietzsche's creative brilliance was apparent at an early age. As a young child he earned the nickname 'little pastor' for his ability to recite scriptural passages and religious songs with great pathos; as a teenager he began to compose poetry and piano, choral and orchestral music; and at 14 he was awarded a scholarship to the outstanding preparatory school in Pforta, with a view to training for the clergy. At school, Nietzsche excelled in religious studies, German literature and classical studies.

In 1861 Nietzsche was confirmed, yet it would be just four years later, during the Easter of 1865, that he would refuse to take communion, much to his family's distress. In 1864 he enrolled at Bonn University to read theology and classical philology (which at that time focused upon the interpretation of classical and biblical texts), but quickly gave up theology and transferred to Leipzig when one of his tutors (Friedrich Ritschl) moved there.

Nietzsche later recalls his excitement around this time at accidentally discovering, in a second-hand bookshop, *The World as Will and Representation* (1818) by the philosopher Arthur Schopenhauer. Schopenhauer's atheistic and chaotic vision of the world, combined with his celebration of music as the highest expression of will, captured Nietzsche's imagination and would come to inspire his own philosophical project.

At university Nietzsche attempted to enter into the student social life (even joining a duelling club), but soon felt himself at a distance from his fellow students as he discovered that his own sense of purpose in life did not match the pursuits and interests of those around him. Nietzsche would come to experience solitude as a necessary condition for creativity.

In 1867 he embarked on his compulsory military service, but his appointment to an equestrian field regiment was curtailed after he acquired a chest wound in attempting to jump into the horse's saddle. He soon returned to the university at Leipzig, where he met Richard Wagner and began a relationship that would prove stormy and heartbreaking for Nietzsche. At this stage, Nietzsche admired Wagner's musical genius and was drawn to his charismatic personality (and shared with him a love of Schopenhauer).

The University of Basel appointed Nietzsche to the chair of classical philology at the extraordinarily young age of 24, before he had received his doctorate. However, the position was not a fruitful one for Nietzsche. He could not strike up friendships with his philology colleagues, but bonded well with other academics there, including the historian Jacob Burkhardt and the theologian Franz Overbeck (who remained a close friend throughout his life, rushing to Nietzsche's aid when he suffered his devastating collapse in 1889). A year later, during the Franco–Prussian war (1870–1), Nietzsche undertook further military service as a hospital attendant. However, he was relieved of his duty after only a few months as a result of contracting diphtheria and dysentery, probably from tending to open wounds of injured soldiers.

Nietzsche's studies in classical philology, together with his reverence for Schopenhauer's philosophy and Wagner's music, as well as his general disdain for Prussian culture, were brought into dialogue in his first book, *The Birth of Tragedy* (1872). Although Wagner lavished praise on it (the second part was devoted to his music), it was heavily criticized in academic circles. Despite the poor reception of *BT*, Nietzsche remained respected in his professional position at Basel University. And at this time he cultivated his friendship with Wagner, and with him he convinced the government to fund the construction of the Bayreuth theatre, which would be dedicated to Wagner's work. The theatre was completed in 1876, and Wagner's self-proclaimed masterpiece, *The Ring of the Nibelung*, was performed for the German Emperor, Wilhelm I. However, much to his despair, Nietzsche despised Wagner's composition and began to question Wagner's ideals (particularly his anti-Semitism). The end of their friendship deeply affected Nietzsche, no doubt contributing to his melancholia. In 1879, at the age of 34, he was forced to resign from his post at Basel due to his deteriorating health, which manifested itself in migraine headaches, insomnia, vomiting, stomach complaints and poor eyesight.

As early as 1869 Nietzsche had given up his Prussian citizenship, and not having obtained Swiss citizenship he remained stateless, preferring instead the life of a wandering scholar. With funds acquired from his retirement pension, he travelled almost annually between his mother's house in Naumburg and various French, German, Swiss and Italian cities, never settling at one place for more than six months at a time. Nietzsche thought that extreme climates exacerbated the symptoms of his ill-health, and to counteract this he often spent his summers in the coolness of the Swiss alpine village of Sils-Maria, and his winters in the French seaside resort of Nice. On one of his visits to Rome in 1882, when Nietzsche was 37, he met and fell in love with Lou Andreas-Salomé, a 21-year-old enigmatic Russian woman and student of philosophy and theology. Salomé rejected two marriage proposals from Nietzsche, and instead accepted one from Nietzsche's friend, Paul Rée. Nietzsche was devastated by her rejection. Salomé later became an associate of Sigmund Freud, and wrote of her psychological insight into Nietzsche's personality, claiming Nietzsche to have been obsessed with God throughout his life.

In his nomadic existence we find Nietzsche living out his philosophical search for creativity in the plurality of perspectives and resistance to settlement. And his productive output in his nomadic years is testimony to the validity and worth of his rootlessness, for it provided the occasion for the writing of 11 of his works. Yet as Nietzsche was all too aware, both intellectually and personally, creativity is a dangerous venture. With it come the misery of isolation and the absence of security and certainty – aspects Nietzsche sought to affirm in his philosophical project yet could not accept in his own life. In a letter of 1887 to his friend Overbeck, he reveals that 'it hurts frightfully that in these 15 years not one single person has "discovered" me, has needed me, has loved me'. Nietzsche was compelled to live an isolated life, without the intimacy of the companionship he so craved. He sought continually to write, despite – or indeed precisely because of – the fact that his ideas failed to attract an interested audience beyond his small circle of friends.

Nietzsche's productivity ended on the morning of 3 January 1889 in Turin, when he suffered a mental breakdown that incapacitated him up to his death in 1900. Reports claim that upon seeing a coachman cruelly whipping his horse, Nietzsche threw his arms around the horse's neck and sobbed uncontrollably before collapsing in the street. The original diagnosis of his illness was a syphilitic infection contracted either as a student or while serving as a hospital attendant in the Franco–Prussian war. Some claim, however, that it was caused by a brain disorder inherited from his father; and others that it was a mental illness that gradually drove him insane, the expressions of which can, apparently, be traced in his work, months before his collapse.[3]

After a brief hospitalization in Basel, Nietzsche spent a year in an asylum in Jena and thereafter was cared for by his mother in Naumburg. After her death in 1897, his sister Elisabeth assumed responsibility for both Nietzsche's welfare and, as we have already noted, the twisted dark myth that surrounds his work. In order to promote her brother's work, Elisabeth rented a large house in Weimar (which became the home of the Nietzsche Archives), to which she moved both her paralysed brother and his manuscripts. Elisabeth invited visitors to the house to observe her brother in his paralytic state and, later, his dead body. On 25 August 1900, Nietzsche died in Weimar, apparently of pneumonia coupled with a stroke.

1

Antichrist versus anti-life

Nietzsche is not in league with the devil. Yet a *superficial* reading of the controversy surrounding Nietzsche the man and his works may well substantiate this ridiculous but not uncommon misconception. It is all too easy to brand Nietzsche a person of malevolent intent, on the basis that he proclaimed the death of God and maliciously attacked Christianity. Add to this his unfortunate endorsement by the Nazi party and the fact that Nietzsche refers to himself as the Antichrist, and you have all the ingredients for notoriety. However, to call Nietzsche demonic is simply ignorant melodrama.

Nietzsche's use and endorsement of the term 'Antichrist' is not to be understood in Christian terms (as the devil in opposition to Christ) but as the antithesis of all that is Christian. In other words, his intention is not to embody or align himself with the Christian notion of evil (indeed, Nietzsche seeks a position *beyond* – good and – evil) but with all that stands in opposition to the Christian tradition. In this sense, it might be more accurate to refer to Nietzsche's position as 'anti-Christianity' rather than Antichrist.

Far from harbouring evil and malevolent intentions, Nietzsche aspires to innocence and honesty, and to that which affirms and enables life. The enhancement of life underpins his philosophy. Commentators have gone so far as to claim that he extols a 'religion' of life or has 'faith' in life. Certainly Nietzsche makes it his concern to expose and denigrate those values and systems of thought that impose on life and simulate control of it. It seems, for Nietzsche, there is nothing greater than life itself, and we, as participants within life, would do well to recognize its value and regard nothing – not even ourselves – as superior to it.

We shall soon see how Nietzsche takes issue with the idea that there are objective truths, which tell us how things really are, and imperatives, which tell us how we ought to behave. According to Nietzsche, truth is contingent and a matter of perspective – so that what is true for you may not be true for me. Nietzsche's philosophical project does not aspire to the definitive explanation of how the world really is or ought to be; rather it explains how the world appears to him. And it argues that we would do well to determine how the world appears to us, and whether this conception is enabling or inhibiting us. Nevertheless, we could argue that it is, for Nietzsche, a 'moral duty' to affirm life and enhance its nature. Furthermore, life seems to take on divine status for Nietzsche, in the pantheistic sense that life is inescapably here, within us and our world, and should not be worshipped or regarded as something transcendent and beyond us.

In this chapter we shall see how Nietzsche attacks Christianity for what he believes are its crimes against life. In particular, for setting itself up in contradistinction to life, with its promise – through death – of a better world beyond human life. We shall see how he regards Christianity as a delusory system of thought that manipulates human life according to its own power-hungry ends. In proclaiming Christianity a 'blasphemy against life' (*TI*, 'Morality as anti-nature' 5), Nietzsche leads us to think that Christianity has offended his own religious sensibilities.

Nietzsche's position of anti-Christianity is a response and reaction to Christianity's position of anti-life. In the course of this chapter the accusation of notoriety will switch from Nietzsche (the misunderstood Antichrist) to Christianity (apparent advocate of anti-life). We shall survey Christianity's betrayal of life, as Nietzsche sees it, through the several ways in which it attempts – through its desire to establish itself as a system of truth – to demolish humanity in order to rebuild it in its own image.

In the section that immediately follows we shall outline the contrasting epistemological concerns that divide Nietzsche and Christianity, as he understands it, which set the scene for Nietzsche's assault on Christianity. We shall find Nietzsche's life-affirming philosophy rooted in what he calls 'the will to power', and Christianity, by contrast, entrenched in a delusory 'will to truth'.

Different responses to life: the will to power and the will to truth

The will to power

Nietzsche regarded life and its experiences as a dynamic interplay of opposing forces, creating conflict and tension. The wrestling of opposing forces exhibits the discord necessary for all existence: 'everything that happens, happens in accordance with this strife' (*PTAG* 5). Nietzsche's view is influenced heavily by the pre-Socratic philosopher Heraclitus, whose thought he revered. Heraclitus viewed the world as in a state of continual flux, so that everything that seems permanent ('being') is simply change in slow motion (or 'becoming'). All structures and established values undergo slow dissolution and alteration; they are, Heraclitus says, 'coming-to-be and passing away'.

This may seem a pessimistic view of life, and Nietzsche believes that it is partly because some of us find such a view intolerable that we inevitably try to defend ourselves against it and adopt a radically different view – one that is grounded in comfortable illusion. Nietzsche believes that many of us need and desire permanent structures of meaning, and that this need drives us towards projecting illusory structures on to the flux of reality in order to hide its meaningless nature. As we shall see, Nietzsche regards Christianity as an example of this deluded response to life. But before we examine exactly how he does so, it is important to note that Heraclitus' view of life – which Nietzsche later develops – is not wholly negative and unconstructive. Indeed, Heraclitus posits the existence in nature of what he calls a hidden 'latent order' (*harmonia*) (Fragment 54) or 'one divine law' (Fragment 114) that masters all events. This latent order or law does not change, but incites change in the world through the cultivation of tensions between opposing forces. It is, Heraclitus says, that which influences and shapes our temporary values. Nietzsche describes the law proposed by Heraclitus as a process – 'the diverging of a force into two qualitatively different opposed activities that seek to re-unite' (*PTAG* 5). In Nietzschean terms, we can understand this law as the 'will to power'. The will to power can therefore be construed as the underlying law of life, which harnesses its tensions to enable 'new and more powerful births'. Put simply, 'life *is* will to power' (*BGE* 259). Indeed, for Nietzsche,

> Our entire instinctual life [is] the development and ramification of *one* basic form of will – as will to power . . . [O]ne [can] trace all organic functions back to this will to power and [can] also find in it the solution to the problem of procreation and nourishment. (*BGE* 36)

Nietzsche calls us, as active participants within life, to promote life's dynamic nature within us. Thus, the will to power describes both life in general and the means by which we engage with life and facilitate its dynamic cycle of creation and destruction within us. Will to power affirms life through the enhancement of opposing activities or values. But this does not mean that one particular activity or value need prevail and dominate its contrasting counterpart, for this would give rise to an established hierarchy of values and ideals. Rather, will to power seeks to enable the tension and creative dialogue between opposites, 'like wrestlers of whom sometimes the one, sometimes the other, is on top' (*PTAG* 5), so that a multitude of perspectives and values are sought and played off against each other, which, in turn, inspires further ideas and values.

Nietzsche seeks human growth – not in a particular direction according to a fixed ideal, in relation to which we inevitably feel unfulfilled, but rather in terms of infinite possibility and perspective, whereby we continually shape and reshape who we are, overcoming ourselves again and again. 'One is *fruitful*', Nietzsche tells us, 'only at the cost of being rich in contradictions; one remains *young* only on condition the soul does not relax, does not long for peace' (*TI*, 'Morality as anti-nature' 3). To endure the immediate chaos of existence requires immense mental strength. The will to power requires us to create a sense of order and form from out of the chaos of conflicting impulses in such a way that no shape is formalized or firmly established: simply to 'impose upon becoming the *character* of being – that is the supreme will to power' (*WP* 617).

'The impermanence of everything actual', which 'comes-to-be but never is', is a 'terrible, paralyzing thought' (*PTAG* 5) that tests our mental strength. Life appears as an amoral game, ready to deceive (*PTAG* 6); it aims to destroy us and everything else that seeks identity, form and shape. Incredibly, Nietzsche says we should not respond to this state of affairs with an attitude that is 'gloomy, melancholy, tearful, sombre, bilious, pessimistic and altogether hateful' (*PTAG* 7). Instead, we should adopt a response similar to that endorsed by the early Greeks, who were able to affirm joyfully the horror of life in its devastation. In Greek tragedy, suffering is transcended by an affirmation of the life-force behind it – an affirmation that despite every phenomenological change, life is at bottom joyful and powerful, so that in its very expression:

> nature cries to us with its true, undissembled voice: 'Be as I am! Amid the ceaseless flux of phenomena I am the eternally creative primordial mother, eternally impelling to existence, eternally finding satisfaction in this change of phenomena!'
>
> (*BT* 16)

Nietzsche's faith in life is incredibly difficult to sustain. Not only does it require expertise in the will to power (an ability continually to redefine our values and reshape chaotic flux – a task of endurance and frustration), it also requires the joyous celebration of chaos. No doubt the majority of us respond to this in the very manner Nietzsche advises against. Indeed, in Chapter 3 we shall see how such a faith in life and will to power is reserved for the elite few: for what Nietzsche calls the *Übermenschen*. For the rest of us, Nietzsche prescribes a different approach to life – one that attempts to escape from it into the illusory world of manufactured 'objective' truth and structured meaning. In contrast to the 'will to power', Nietzsche calls this approach to life the 'will to truth'.

The will to truth

It is much easier for the majority of us to believe in a reality different from the one postulated by Nietzsche and by Heraclitus before him. That is to say, we are more likely to posit a *purposeful* reality that is grounded in ultimate meaning, as opposed to the blind chaos of meaninglessness. If you approach life with a will to truth, you are more likely to experience life in the comfort of certainty than in the horror of its insecurity. With certainty, however, comes limitation. Thus, while the will to power regards human life as one of infinite possibility, the will to truth considers it lived according to a perceived fixed ideal, against which the person is judged and valued. The will to truth therefore withholds its full appreciation of human life until the perceived ideal or goal of that life has been realized. A person is not regarded as an end in itself, but as a means to something more valuable and rewarding. While the will to power enables us to engage the fullness of life, the will to truth shuts it out. While the former demands heroism, strength and conscious affirmation, the latter requires unconscious submission, a weakness of will and repressed creativity. Therefore those who would rather seek comfort, peace and safety in the community of truths and values (an approach Nietzsche calls 'herd'-thinking) than in the tension and strife of individual creation may find themselves happy, but they can never be satisfied (*WP* 696). Such people, Nietzsche says, 'become nothing' (*HAH* 626), because they are incapable of creative development and self-overcoming. They do not *live*; they fear life, and abstract themselves from it.

One reason why Nietzsche attacks Christianity is because it is a manifestation of the will to truth. Christianity is, he thinks, a delusional value-system that negates human life because it regards itself as the source of ultimate meaning that lies outside life. Far from being a genuine means of overcoming nihilism, Nietzsche regards Christianity as its very expression (*WP* 156) because it negates the meaningfulness of human life by relocating the source of meaning beyond life.[1]

According to Nietzsche, Christianity, like its metaphysical precursor, Platonic philosophy, is a projection of human fear in the face of continual change. Both seek to save humanity from the horrors of change by uniting humanity with that which cannot change: ultimate truth. While Plato's project can be conceived as an attempt to escape the contingencies of fortune (which the philosopher Martha Nussbaum calls the 'fragility of goodness') by finding in the world of 'Forms' a ground of value that is self-sufficient and immune from change and chance (where goodness is not fragile), Christianity seeks to rescue humanity from its finite world in order to resituate it in an eternal, unchanging world with God. The Christian and Platonic conceptions both value the non-dynamic, changeless world over and above the life of flux of the here and now. For Nietzsche this conception of a static world is severed from life, for anything that does not change cannot grow and cannot *live*, and is thus indistinguishable from death. The price of safety from the horror of life is death. For Nietzsche, the Christian and Platonic celebration of a world beyond change and time is a divinization of death and nihilism. To put it another way, the problem with Christianity for Nietzsche is that it severs human life from that which makes it what it is. And a soteriology conceived on these grounds is what the Nietzsche scholar Giles Fraser aptly calls 'metaphysical suicide'.

Christianity and Platonism therefore make engagement with life impossible because they deny life in favour of an abstract, illusory world beyond it. Nietzsche attacks both Christianity and Platonism for conceiving an absurd and ascetic dualism – whereby (finite, human) life is pitted in opposition to (eternal) meaning, so that meaning is determined at the expense of life. The dualism is further enhanced by their common insistence on placing the value of reason above instinct. Salvation in the security of the Christian God or the Platonic world of Forms is enabled through rational contemplation and the eradication of desires (which are deemed within these models to be transitory and unreliable aspects of the contingent and finite world). Just as Nietzsche calls us to facilitate the changing nature of life itself within ourselves by adopting the will to power, Christianity and Platonism effectively call us to emulate the dualistic nature of reality. Thus, the Christian advocates the contrast between the divinized world of permanence and the denigrated human world of flux by splitting his or her own nature into a revered rational aspect (reason is revered because it leads us to certainty and objective truth) and a devalued emotional one (emotions are devalued because their fleeting nature leads us astray into subjective indulgence). Christianity creates a dualism within the fabric of life that cannot be reconciled. Its goal is to escape life and to be redeemed from it, and this is achievable if one is able to affirm the 'correct' half of the division and denigrate the other. Christianity is thus incapable of promoting life to the full, and can only extol its fragmentation.

Physiological engagement with life

Life for Nietzsche is not an abstract concept for us to reflect upon and deconstruct according to our intellectual prejudices. It is, rather, an embodied experience that engages our non-rational instincts as much as our reason. Nietzsche's philosophy cannot be separated from physiology and psychology. Thus, the value of life cannot be assessed by external criteria or from an impartial, objective standpoint, as no such criteria or perspectives exist. Likewise, the value of life cannot be discovered through the rational contemplation of Platonic Forms or of God's enduring love. Rather, the value of life for Nietzsche is discovered at every moment in which it is experienced here and now, and as an end in itself. The value of life is in the living of it. The meaning of life cannot be encapsulated in thought, but in body. Life isn't determined in its abstract contemplation, it is an ever-present, ceaseless activity. Indeed, as we saw in the introduction to this book, Nietzsche claims that there is no 'meaning' or 'truth' of life to discover, for 'our most sacred convictions, the unchanging elements in our supreme values, are judgements of our muscles' (*WP* 314).

Physiological constitution plays a large part in Nietzsche's critique of Christianity and in his philosophy in general. To embrace life to its fullest is to *embody* life. The will to power, as that which enables life, can be likened to a muscle that flexes and strengthens as it engages with the strife it is confronted with. To use an expression from common parlance, the will to power enables us to 'stomach' life. To be strong and powerful, for Nietzsche, is not to dominate life but to master our response to the strife that life presents. It is to create out of chaos and, as Nietzsche suggests, even to dance on the edge of the abyss. By contrast, the will to truth is weak precisely because it seeks to dominate and control life by imposing structure and purpose upon it. This is a delusional form of power, a projection of weakness. The person who employs the will to truth has a weak constitution for life; he or she needs as a crutch the delusional belief that reality is coming to his or her rescue with formulas of salvation. As Nietzsche's fictional character Zarathustra (with whom we shall familiarize ourselves in the next chapter) laments: 'impotence . . . created all afterworlds . . . [T]he sick and dying . . . invented the things of heaven and the redeeming drops of blood' (*TSZ*, 'Of the afterworldsmen'). Unfortunately, we can have no influence on the strength of our constitution: whether we are strong enough to adopt the will to power or so weak that we submit to a will to truth is predetermined by our physiological disposition. Thus, Nietzsche claims, 'No one is free to become a Christian or not to do so; one is not "converted" to Christianity – one must be sufficiently sick for it' (*AC* 51). Those of us who adopt the will to truth forfeit the opportunity to create, develop and individuate.

We will 'become nothing' because we are nourished by delusions and not by life. By contrast, those of us who adopt the will to power embody what Nietzsche refers to as 'great health' (*GS* 382).

Several of Nietzsche's ideas anticipate those of psychoanalytic theory, and his criterion for sickness and health is a good case in point. Thus health, for Nietzsche, is a matter of enabling dialogue between conflicting impulses and of channelling (or sublimating) the energy generated by this conflict into creative expression. Illness, on the other hand, occurs when conflicting impulses do not enter into dialogue, so that one impulse is utilized and the other is denied its conscious expression. A consequence of having denied or repressed this impulse is that it is subsequently projected outside of the self on to another person or object, where it is experienced as an autonomous entity in its own right, rather than as a disowned aspect of the self.

Both Nietzsche and psychoanalysts are in the business of exposing those delusions we invent to protect ourselves from difficult and potentially destructive 'home truths'. Just as the psychoanalyst attempts to make the unconscious conscious, Nietzsche seeks to uncover the hidden agendas and underlying motivations of established belief-systems. Likewise, just as psychoanalytic therapy aims to heal the patient by reintegrating disowned aspects back into his or her conscious self, Nietzsche's project can be construed as an attempt to deconstruct manifestations of the will to truth in order to prompt the withdrawal of their value-projections on to the world, so that conceptions of the world can be healed from their life-denying restrictions.

Analysis of a belief-system that is projected on to life by the will to truth will reveal the particular concerns and needs of the believer – most significantly, it will expose what the believer feels he or she needs to believe in order to feel in control of life. Nietzsche attempted to do just this by exposing the physiological 'origin of our moral prejudices' (*GM*, Preface

2), with particular focus on the genealogical development of Christianity. As we shall see, his analysis concludes that Christianity, as a system of beliefs, is a manifestation of a chronic sickness, the principal symptom of which is an obsessive desire for power. After we have outlined Nietzsche's diagnosis of Christianity as a disease, we shall turn our attention to St Paul, whom Nietzsche singles out as the most sick – and infectious – Christian of all.

Diagnosing Christianity

According to Nietzsche, Christianity is a disease that spreads hatred for human life. To assist in the spread of its infection it has invented and beatified a set of corrupt and corrupting valuations, which include sin, guilt, pity, cruelty, 'good' and 'evil', and constitute what Nietzsche refers to as 'slave morality'. Nietzsche diagnoses Christianity as a chronic disease, because he thinks it has been infecting Western civilization for almost 2,000 years, and will continue to do so (at least until we can effectively sustain what Nietzsche calls a 'revaluation of values'; in Chapter 3 we shall see what this entails). One reason for the prolonged infection of Christianity is due to its addictive nature. According to Nietzsche, Christianity is an addictive drug that promotes itself as a cure. The Christian priest, he says, is rather like a manipulative quack or fraudulent physician, who administers the illusion of cure:

> He [the priest] brings salves and balm with him, no doubt; but before he can act as a physician he first has to wound; when he then stills the pain of the wound *he at the same time infects the wound* – for that is what he knows how to do best of all.
>
> (*GM* III 15)

The ascetic priest is as infected with the physiological deficiencies as those he treats. He has opportunistic investment in and talent for controlling and manipulating the sickness by

11

merely managing and directing the symptoms rather than removing their underlying cause.

For Nietzsche, Christianity is both a genuine sickness and an illusory cure. The Christian's 'cure', as Nietzsche conceives it (as redemption and salvation from the human condition), is totally irrelevant and inane, for if there is no sin there is no need for salvation. Nietzsche claims that Christianity has invented 'nothing but imaginary *causes*' – such as, 'God', 'soul', 'ego', 'spirit', 'free will' – and 'nothing but imaginary *effects*' – including, 'sin', 'redemption', 'grace', 'punishment' and 'forgiveness of sins' (*AC* 15). It also creates a dangerous and unnecessary paradox: 'the nihilism of salvation' which, as Giles Fraser notes, asserts that life is meaningful if and only if there exists a non-worldly realm that invests human life with significance. Without God life is meaningless. And the more Christianity is able to promote life as meaningless the more it is able to promote God as the saviour of life.[2]

What is the motivation behind this needless paradox? Nietzsche claims that it is the need for power. If we recall, he says that everything strives for power (life *is* will to power); even those of weak constitution desire the power they do not have. Unable to exercise the positive power *of* life, weak-willed people seek the negative power *over* life: an unworldly, anti-life power. They seek not 'will to power' but the illusion of power. The Christian God, then, is simply a projection of ultimate power to provide a crutch for its impotent believers, who are incapable of harnessing the power of life for themselves. Power is claimed for the Christian not through his or her own weak will, but in the idea of the 'ultimate' power of a divine will to which they submit themselves. The Christian projects or

> ejects from himself all denial of himself, of his nature, naturalness and actuality, in the form of an affirmation, as something existent, corporeal, real, as God, as the holiness of God, as God the Judge, as God the Hangman, as the beyond, as eternity, as torment without end, as hell, as the immeasurability of punishment and guilt. (*GM* II 22)

In other words, to have faith in the utter power and holiness of God is, Nietzsche would maintain, a mere compensation for the denial of one's own utter impotence.

And the Christian ideal does not stop at simply raising the power-status of the weak: it also wants to undercut the status of the strong and noble. Nietzsche describes these power struggles in terms of a revolt of 'slave morality' against 'master morality'. Whereas master morality is the expression of 'a powerful physicality, a blossoming, rich, even effervescent good health' (*GM* I 7), slave morality is the manifestation of a sickly, all-consuming hatred, which Nietzsche calls *ressentiment* (a notion that will be discussed later in this chapter). We shall now turn to these moral types described by Nietzsche to outline their differences and explain how slave morality both underpins Christian thought and has come to dominate Western culture generally.

Master morality and slave morality

Morality, for Nietzsche, describes the way we structure and order our lives. As we have seen, Nietzsche rejects the existence of structures that objectively determine the meaning of our lives, claiming them to be illusory projections of a weak will. Thus, he says, 'There are no moral phenomena at all, only moral interpretations of phenomena' (*BGE* 108). Nietzsche's understanding of morality is completely at odds with the Kantian notion of a universal and a priori rational law. Morality, as Nietzsche sees it, is simply those values and meanings that prevail in a given time or place. They cannot endure permanently or categorically, but come into being and pass away.

Despite such moral fluidity, Nietzsche describes two fundamental and opposing moral 'types' or tendencies, which – although co-existent in every culture and personality in different degrees – struggle to dominate each other in order to facilitate the development of moral values. He refers to the two types as 'master' and 'slave' morality. Their distinction underpins much of Nietzsche's thought, and is discussed most explicitly in the first essay of *On the Genealogy of Morals* (1887). It is important to note, however, that although Nietzsche regards Christianity as an expression of slave morality par excellence, nowhere does he endorse master morality as the ideal human approach to life, as is commonly supposed. He is certainly more critical of slave morality, but this is most likely due to his belief that slave morality is a greater threat to modern society. Nietzsche seeks a revaluation of values in order to rebalance the modern tendency towards slavish values, to which end the value of master morality must be emphasized. We shall now briefly outline these moral tendencies in turn.

Master morality describes a life shaped by the will to power. It is a morality of noble sentiment and strength, of deciding what is useful for the furtherance of creativity and life. What is helpful to the strong-willed person is that which enables his or her growth and self-overcoming. Master morality, then, is an affirmation of self as the measure of all things:

> The noble type of man feels *himself* to be the determiner of values, he does not need to be approved of, he judges, 'what harms me is harmful in itself', he knows himself to be that which in general first accords honour to things, he *creates values.*
> (*BGE* 260; cf. *GM* I 11)

The good is, therefore, whatever I value in myself. Goodness is identified with values of self-worth and self-confidence, such as nobility, intelligence, strength, courage, honesty, loyalty and open-mindedness. Badness, by contrast, is simply a corollary. It is that which is not good. Badness is identified with all that hinders the development of the person and stunts his or her growth. Badness is thus all that is weak, cowardly, timid and petty.

Slave morality, on the other hand, stands for all that master morality is not. Slave morality turns master morality on its head, making virtues out of the master's conception of badness and vices out of the master's goodness. By inverting the master's values, the slave is able to villainize the master and declare him immoral. While master morality is determined by sentiment, Nietzsche tells us that slave morality finds motivation in resentment (or, rather, what Nietzsche refers to as *ressentiment*, and the revaluation of that which the master values). Slave morality attempts to undermine the master and make him a slave too, rather than overpower him and transcend his worth. Slave morality approaches life with scepticism and pessimism, seeking to vanquish those who affirm life and create in its name.

Whereas masters are creators of morality, slaves can only derive their values from the master's creation. Likewise, slaves are dependent on the master for their existence and sense of power, for the negative power that motivates the weak slave cannot manifest itself spontaneously; it is only ever drawn from something more powerful and self-sufficient. Slaves feed off their masters like parasites, always deriving their values from their reactions to their powerful masters. And slaves are power-hungry! For Nietzsche claims that those who do not have power seek to obtain it from those who do. Delusional Christians exemplify this slavish and desperate desire for power by affiliating themselves with an omnipotent God. Nietzsche writes:

> Faith is always coveted most and needed most urgently where will is lacking; for will [has] the affect of command . . . [T]he less one knows how to command, the more urgently one covets someone who commands, who commands severely – a god, prince, class, physician, father confessor, dogma or party conscience. (*GS* 347)

The weak gain power by corrupting the strong into believing that those values of strength to which the weak cannot subscribe are in fact 'evil'. In regarding such principles as humility, meekness, pity and charity as unconditional virtues to which we all must aspire, slave morality avoids having to admit that they are actually conditions forced upon slaves by their masters.

Biblical principles of charity and love for thy neighbour are the result of universalizing the quandary of the slave, thereby making slaves of us all. Nietzsche regarded democracy and Christianity as the same emasculating impulse, which seeks to constrain individuality by making us all slaves to equality, and to suppress the creativity that is born of tensions of difference.

The rise of slave morality and the spread of infection

Of course 'slave' and 'master', as fundamental moral 'types', are not intended by Nietzsche to be abstract, ideological formulas. Rather, he claims that they are perceived as historical trends that have shaped the development of cultural values. Nietzsche traces historically the slave revolt and rise to power of slavish values through his conception of the Christian tradition and its development. As a slave morality, Christianity is fuelled by the negative power of *ressentiment*. Thus, we will find that Nietzsche's historical survey is also an explanation of how *ressentiment* came to infect the West, and led to '*the collective degeneration of man*' (*BGE* 127). Let us now turn to his survey.

Nietzsche reveres ancient Greek and Roman societies for extolling the principles of master morality. Since the ancient Greeks were able to affirm joyously the tragedy and horror of life, it seems appropriate that the Homeric heroes, the 'men of noble culture' (*BGE* 153), are they who epitomize the strong-willed men. Nietzsche also finds in the Romans suitable representatives, as they are 'the strongest and most noble people who ever lived' (*GM* I 16). Pitted in opposition to the Roman master is the Judaean slave. In Nietzsche's historical reading of events, it was the occasion of Jewish Exile that instigated humanity's downfall and a subsequent change in moral outlook from master morality to slave morality. The defeat of master morality was confirmed when Christianity was born as a delusional crutch for the Judaean slave, and subsequently flourished and spread like an infection throughout the Roman Empire. Nietzsche writes,

> [T]he Jews achieved that miracle of inversion of values thanks to which life on earth has for a couple of millennia acquired a new and dangerous fascination – their prophets fused 'rich', 'godless', 'evil', 'violent', 'sensual' into one and were the first to coin the word 'world' as a term of infamy. It is this inversion of values (with which is involved the employment of the word for 'poor' as a synonym for 'holy' and 'friend') that the significance of the Jewish people resides: with *them* there begins the *slave revolt in morals.* (*BGE* 118)

Nietzsche's historical critique is outlined in two places. In *On the Genealogy of Morals* he discusses the rise of slave morality with fleeting reference to Hebrew history, where the Jews are portrayed as a weak tribe superseded by the noble warrior tribes of the ancient world. In *The Anti-Christ* his allusions to Hebrew history are more detailed, complex and difficult to follow. This latter account differentiates between the pre- and post-Exilic Jews in order to chart the demise of Hebrew history from its heights with the noble pre-Exilic Jew, to its lows in the slavish Christian. Nietzsche, therefore, does not equate the entire Jewish tradition with 'weakness', but a certain type of Jew: the post-Exilic, priestly type. (Similarly, as we shall see in the final chapter, Nietzsche does not attack *all* Christians *in toto*; he in fact reveres what he calls the 'most serious Christian'.) Indeed, the pre-Exilic Jew is highly respected by Nietzsche and, generally speaking, so is the Torah:

> [A]ll honour to the Old Testament! I find in it great human beings, a heroic landscape, and something of the very rarest quality in the world, the incomparable naïveté of the *strong heart*; what is more, I find a people. (*GM* III 22)

By contrast, Nietzsche denigrates its Christian counterpart, the New Testament, for portraying a very different quality of life, one squalid and poor and 'equivalent to a Russian novel'. The Hebrew people are seen by Nietzsche to enjoy and celebrate life because they were able to live *beyond good and evil* – at a time before these moral parameters were cultivated and established in the Christian tradition.

According to Nietzsche, the Jewish people, prior to their Exile, affirmed life through a noble morality:

> Originally, above all in the period of the Kingdom, Israel stood in a correct, that is to say natural relationship to all things. Their Yahweh was the expression of their consciousness of power, of their delight in themselves, their hopes of themselves: in him they anticipated victory and salvation, with him they trusted that nature would provide what the people needed – above all rain. (*AC* 25)

Nietzsche argues that the Hebrew god was a positive projection of the Jewish people. Yahweh mirrored back to them an image of who and what they were and who and what they could be. This self-affirmation and confidence in life were dependent on the contingency of good fortune; but the Jewish people were unfortunate enough to be conquered by the Babylonians, which resulted in the enforced relocation of its more prominent citizens from Judah to the city of Babylon. This defeat proved devastating for the Jews, not least because Hebrew history was structured around the promise of Yahweh to protect the Jewish people and to use them for his own purpose. The defeat and subsequent loss of land promised to them by Yahweh seemed to invalidate his promise and their faith in him. Yet, for Nietzsche, the devastation of this historic defeat reached far beyond the despairing Jews – it inspired the catastrophic downfall of modern humanity as a whole. Nietzsche claims that in order to make sense of Yahweh's apparent inability to keep a promise, the Jewish priests invented the notion of sin. The invention of sin meant that Yahweh was absolved of all blame for the Jewish Exile, as this responsibility and fault could now be deflected on to the Jewish people themselves: they were exiled as a divine *punishment* for their sins. Nietzsche concedes that the Hebrew conception of a god of flourishing land and fulfilment of national hopes was no longer feasible; but that did not justify, for him, the monstrous replacement for this obsolete god. The loss of the very foundation of the

Jewish belief-system precipitated profound despair and a fundamental restructuring of that system. The Jewish revaluation of values would become a reversal of those values celebrated in pre-Exilic culture. Far from affirming life, the new value-system was founded on the very despair and misery that instigated its conception. The enslaved Jewish people advocated a 'slave morality' that celebrated the very hatred of life.

The invention of sin

According to Nietzsche, sin is a clever story invented by the Jewish priests to explain and justify their enslavement, as well as a clever political measure to maintain a peaceful society. But such peace, he says, comes at great cost to human life, for sin creates terrible life-denying values, such as *ressentiment*, 'bad conscience', guilt and cruelty. In other words, for Nietzsche, sin symbolizes hatred of humanity; and if one is to sustain an image of a just god, one is forced to hate human life.

The Jews were impelled to find divine purpose in their enslaved condition, and through the doctrine of sin they were able to divinize their powerlessness and make a virtue of their suffering and limitation. The slave's suffering is made purposeful only if he or she is regarded as having done something suitably bad to warrant it. Thus, by redefining human nature as inherently impure, unworthy and sinful, the Jewish priests were able to justify their enslavement and suffering. Put simply, they suffered because they *deserved* to suffer. However, this is not the end to their clever, fabricated story, for divine punishment leads to the possibility of divine forgiveness and redemption from sin. Suffering therefore comes with incentives, and is an attractive proposition because it is the means to salvation and union with God. The Jewish priests interpreted the misfortune of Exile as 'sin' and subsequently replaced what was once a natural world-order with a moral one. Through the invention of sin, the historical foundation of Israel was rewritten in terms, Nietzsche says, of a 'stupid salvation-mechanism of guilt towards Yahweh and punishment, piety towards Yahweh and reward' (*AC* 26).

Nietzsche argues that the qualities and characteristics that were forced upon the slave were reinterpreted as virtues and moral qualities required for salvation. Thus, impotence, submissiveness, apprehensiveness and the inability to create for oneself were reinterpreted as humility, friendliness, patience and solidarity with one's neighbour. But as Nietzsche contends, this revision of values was not conjured up by Jewish priests simply because it helped make theological sense of a desperate situation (of their enslavement). The revision of values was also motivated by anger and revenge against those who instigated the need for it in the first place: against the powerful oppressors. The enslaved Jews sought to give their oppressors a taste of their own medicine, as it were, and make slaves out of them too. But because they were not in a position to assert themselves physically, they resorted to a moral or spiritual revenge with the implementation of their radical reversal of values. Nietzsche writes,

> It was the Jews who, with awe-inspiring consistency . . . declared: 'The wretched alone are the good; the poor, impotent, lowly alone are the good; the suffering, deprived, sick, ugly alone are pious, alone are blessed by God, blessedness is for them alone – and you, the powerful and noble, are on the contrary the evil, the cruel, the lustful, the insatiable, the godless to all eternity; and you shall be in all eternity the unblessed, accursed, and damned!'
> (*GM* I 7)

Christianity later consolidated the spiritual revenge of the slave by postulating a heaven for the meek to inhabit, from where they could view their earthly masters suffering eternally as slaves in hell. Nietzsche notes how theologians, including Tertullian and Aquinas, have taken great enjoyment and pleasure in the suffering of the damned (*GM* I 25). Far from extolling the values of humility, Nietzsche saw the post-Exilic Jewish tradition as advocating enjoyment in the practice of cruelty and hatred of human power. Cruelty enabled the Christian to cultivate a sense of his or her own power and subsequently to forget momentarily their own suffering, which is, Nietzsche argues, a product of their own weakness (*D* 16; *GS* 13). The Christian, in Nietzsche's critique, has what we might call an inferiority complex; and for Nietzsche, the entire Christian moral enterprise is founded upon feelings of inadequacy and the inability to comprehend and accept these feelings for what they are. We shall now attempt to explain how Nietzsche comes to this conclusion by outlining two important concepts in his thought: bad conscience and *ressentiment*.

Bad conscience

The incarceration of the Jewish people meant they could neither affirm nor celebrate life as they had done before. Their instincts no longer enjoyed freedom of expression, and in the absence of a natural outlet their life-affirming instincts were forced into repression. And this Nietzsche saw as a big problem, for the repression of instincts led inadvertently to the formation of the Christian value-system that he vehemently attacked. The trouble with repressed instincts, according to Nietzsche, is that their power or energy does not dissipate as a result of their inhibition; rather it intensifies, becoming 'the most dangerous of explosives' (*GM* III 15). This intensification of power cannot be ignored. Rather, the repressed instinct inevitably finds a way out of its repression and into conscious expression. So, Nietzsche says, through a process of 'internalization',

> All instincts that do not discharge themselves outwardly *turn inward* – this is what I call the *internalization* of man: thus it was that man first developed what was later called his 'soul'.
>
> (*GM* II 16)

In other words, when instincts are repressed they create for themselves an 'inner realm' within the person (similar to the psychoanalytic notion of the unconscious). The creation of this new realm has monumental repercussions in the evolutionary nature of human being, for it signifies the creation of a moral soul to rival the motivations of the natural body – together with an entirely new conception of instinctual motivation, namely, the will to truth in distinction to the will to power of the natural body. Because this realm is a product of inhibition (of life and instinct), Nietzsche construes it as a sickness that leads only to further symptoms of sickness. One major symptom is what Nietzsche calls *bad conscience*:

> The entire inner world, originally as thin as if it were stretched between two membranes, expanded and extended itself, acquired depth, breadth, and height, in the same measure as outward discharge was *inhibited* . . . all those instincts of wild, free, prowling man turned backward *against man himself*. Hostility, cruelty, joy in persecuting, in attacking, in change, in destruction – all this turned against the possessors of such instincts: *that* is the origin of the 'bad conscience'.
>
> (*GM* II 16)

Bad conscience, then, is the internalization of aggressive instincts; that is to say, aggression directed upon the self, or self-hatred. This is not a wholly negative state of affairs. Indeed, Nietzsche compares it to the 'sickness of pregnancy', of 'something so new, profound, unheard of, enigmatic, contradictory, and *pregnant with a future*' (*GM* II 16). Nietzsche therefore does not disparage bad conscience, for it is only in bad conscience that we are capable of inward depth and self-cultivation. Likewise, Nietzsche does not denigrate the architecture of the 'soul' in its own right or attack the notion of 'soul' *in toto*. His disagreement is with a particular type of soul, with the soul that has become perverted; in other words, with the 'moral soul' that houses God. Bad conscience is a volatile condition that can give birth either to glorious creations or terrible ones. For Nietzsche, the most terrible creation or ultimate perversion of bad conscience arises when it is mixed with what he calls *ressentiment*. The union of bad conscience with *ressentiment* gives birth to a 'moral baby', a baby born into sin.

Ressentiment

Ressentiment is a word often used by Nietzsche. It is similar to, but not interchangeable with, the English term 'resentment' or the French '*ressentiment*'. Although all three refer to feelings of frustration at a perceived source, Nietzsche goes further in his meaning of the term by grounding this frustration in a complex relationship between feelings of inferiority and the creation of morality.

In the course of this chapter we have come across *ressentiment* several times within the context of denial and hatred of life. Now we shall describe this negative force in more detail to show how it creates Christian morality from the plight of the enslaved Jews.

Nietzsche describes *ressentiment* as a reactive force that deflects the pain and frustration that accompanies feelings of inferiority away from the self and on to an external substitute. This substitute, or 'scapegoat', is then blamed as the source of the frustration and pain, leaving the self to feel at ease with itself. This blame leads quickly to desire for revenge, as the self feels bitter for the pain the scapegoat has apparently inflicted upon it. The denied feelings of weakness and inferiority of the self (and perhaps jealousy of the other) do not diminish when projected outside the self; they generate a reactive, rejecting and self-justifying value-system or morality, which attacks or negates the scapegoat. An illusory enemy is thus created from the sense of powerlessness so that I conceive myself to be oppressed by an external evil rather than my own weakness.

According to Nietzsche, *ressentiment* is rife in weak people. Because it is a reactive, negative energy, it is unlikely to manifest itself in the active, dynamic, creative person of strong will. Similarly, the strong or noble person is unlikely to reflect on those 'bad' things that have been done to him; and, if he does, his reactions are likely to be short-lived. The weak person, by contrast, is incapable of indifference and is likely to react to any potential threat, and to be preoccupied with it. The enslaved Jew, Nietzsche claims, is full of *ressentiment* and highly reactive, so that he or she projects his or her feelings of weakness on to an imagined 'evil master', who is subsequently blamed for the slave's own limitation and failure. The doctrines of sin and the forgiveness of sins are believed by the enslaved Jew to have been divinely authored; but they are, Nietzsche claims, nothing more than a creation of an embittered mind: a morality devised from weakness and a sickness that seeks to negate the power of the master. Nietzsche describes the sickness of *ressentiment* as 'the most spiritual and poisonous kind of hatred' (*GM* I 7), because it attempts to separate life from humanity in order to bring a sense of relief and illusion of power to those who cannot affirm life for themselves.

According to Nietzsche, priests are the worst perpetrators of *ressentiment* precisely because they 'are the most powerless', and from 'out of this powerlessness, their hate swells into something huge and uncanny to a most intellectual and poisonous level' (*GM* I 7). Priests crave power, and in order to acquire it they 'develop theories of guilt, sin, and forgiveness', which 'allow them to be the mediators of a system of reward and punishment' and to preside over the very fate of humanity. Earlier we saw that Nietzsche portrays the priest as a quack doctor, who administers drugs to heal the illnesses that he himself has engendered. The priests are thus clever manipulators of the weak-minded who promise illusions of healing salvation in order to feed their own power-hungry sickness. The 'Supreme Law: "God forgives him who repents"' – when translated 'in plain language' is, Nietzsche says, simply that which 'submits to the priests' (*AC* 139). Of the priests, he further notes, 'By allowing God to judge they themselves judge; by glorifying God they glorify themselves' (*AC* 158). The most poisonous disease created by the priest is sin, and the drug the priest prescribes to heal it is self-hatred. When *ressentiment* is turned inward, a person becomes obsessed with sin and constantly scrutinizes his or her conscience. The doctrine of sin therefore weakens a person's resolve as it incites continual self-criticism. Moreover, the doctrine of forgiveness of sins is, Nietzsche claims, even more devastating and detrimental to the human spirit because it completely destroys any hope or opportunity for human power. Nietzsche argues that the crucifixion marks the climax of self-hatred insofar as it pronounces human beings inherently useless and powerless. The cross asserts that we can never repay our debt to God, and only God can save us from sin. For Nietzsche, the cross symbolizes death, *ressentiment* and hatred of life.

Paul: the most diseased man

If, for Nietzsche, the exiled Jew is full of *ressentiment*, and the priests are even more so, St Paul represents, for him, the most corrupt of them all. Nietzsche writes:

> On the heels of the 'glad tidings' came the *worst of all*: those of Paul. In Paul was embodied the antithetical type to the 'bringer of glad tidings', the genius of hatred, of the vision of hatred, of the inexorable logic of hatred. (*AC* 42)

Nietzsche singles out Paul as the principal agent of theological corruption: the individual who managed to infect the human race with his anti-life morality, which was born out of deep-seated personal impotence and revengeful *ressentiment*.

Nietzsche's attack on Paul first appears, and in most detail, in *Daybreak*. Here he outlines how Paul's obsession with his inability to fulfil the Jewish law led him to reinterpret the event and meaning of the crucifixion so as to take revenge upon the law. Paul was, Nietzsche says, a 'very tormented, very pitiable, very unpleasant man who also found himself unpleasant' (*D* 68). Although Paul fanatically defended the law and was on constant watch for transgressors of it (whom he would then severely punish), he was clearly frustrated with the law and with his own inability to fulfil its demands. Nietzsche elaborates on those 'many things [that] lay on his conscience – he [Paul] hints at enmity, murder, sorcery, idolatry, uncleanliness, drunkenness and pleasure in debauch'. Nietzsche continues to note:

> However much he tried to relieve this conscience, and even more his lust for domination, through the extremist fanaticism in revering and defending the law, there were moments when he said to himself: 'It is all in vain! The torture of the unfulfilled law cannot be overcome.' (*D* 68)

It would seem, indeed, that Paul lays blame for his weakness at the door of the law itself, for he writes,

> If it had not been for the law, I would not have known sin. I would not have known what it is to covet if the law had not said, 'You shall not covet.' But sin, seizing an opportunity in the commandment, produced in me all kinds of covetousness.
> (Romans 7.7–8)

And Paul certainly appears to be full of self-hatred, as he regards himself as the 'Wretched man that I am!' and asks, 'Who will rescue me from this body of death?' (Romans 7.24). In the absence of an obvious redeemer, Nietzsche believes that Paul invents one – one who is willing to substitute his own body of death for that of Paul and those of the entire human race. And Jesus of Nazareth was an obvious candidate upon whom Paul could project his ideas. The disciples of Jesus had expected that he would set up his kingdom on earth, but his premature death had prevented him from doing so. According to Nietzsche, Paul saw immediately how he could cash in on these events and manipulate them so as to take out his revenge against the law, which he had come to resent so much. Nietzsche maintains, therefore, that Paul took it upon himself to conjure up a theological explanation for the given fact of Jesus' death; and since Paul could not find an explanation in Jesus' life, Nietzsche says he made one up: '[F]rom the facts of Christ's life and death [Paul] made a quite arbitrary selection, *giving everything a new accentuation*' (*WP* 167). Paul recasts Jesus as Christ, the messiah: the one who will rescue Paul and the human race from the law and from sin. Thus, in Paul Nietzsche finds the 'First Christian' and 'inventor of Christianism' (*D* 68).

Nietzsche interprets Paul's vision on the road to Damascus not as a vision of Christ but of how to overcome the law:

> What essentially happened then is rather this: his *mind* suddenly became clear: 'it is *unreasonable*,' he says to himself, 'to perse-cute precisely this Christ! For here is the way out, here is perfect revenge, here and nowhere else do I have and hold the *destroyer of the law*!' ... The tremendous consequences of this notion, this solution of the riddle, whirl before his eyes, all at once he is the happiest of men.　　　(*D* 68)

And he is happy, Nietzsche asserts, because he has found a way to overcome his impotence and acquire power. Nietzsche describes Paul as having a 'lust for domination' (*D* 68), and the Christ and God that 'Paul invented for himself' are products of his lust; they represent 'in reality only the resolute *deter-mination* of Paul himself' (*AC* 47).

One of Paul's major weaknesses of character is, Nietzsche suggests, his need continually to *explain* things. In a note of 1888 Nietzsche writes,

> Toward a psychology of Paul – The given fact is the death of Jesus. This has to be explained – That an explanation may be true or false has never entered the minds of such people as these: one day a sublime possibility comes into their heads; 'this death *could* mean such and such' – and at once it *does* mean such and such! A hypothesis is proved true by the sublime impetus it imparts to its originator – 'The proof of power': i.e., an idea is proved true by its effect ... what inspires must be true.　　　(*WP* 171)

Thus, Paul's vision on the road to Damascus demonstrates how his realization that Jesus' death can be explained in such a way as to overcome the law gives rise to a newly found sense of power within him. And this sublime and powerful effect in turn causes Paul to believe that his explanation is true. It would seem that Paul is pathologically motivated by the need to *explain*: to turn facts into interpretations. Nietzsche sees this in evidence in Paul's treatment of Jesus' death.

After learning of the spread of corruption found by Nie-tzsche in the Judaeo-Christian world – from exiled Jew, priest and St Paul – it may come as a surprise also to learn that Nietzsche held the person and life of Jesus in high regard. In Chapter 3 we shall outline this in more detail (where we will place Nietzsche's impression of Jesus in close proximity to his conceptions of the higher man and free spirit); but for now it is important simply to note that Nietzsche saw in Jesus a noble affirmer of life and, subsequently, the *imitatio Christi* as a not unworthy way to conduct one's own life. Earlier we saw how Nietzsche valued life in the living of it rather than any explanation of it; here we find the point exemplified by Jesus' life. Thus, Nietzsche maintains that the value of Jesus' life is in its imitation, not its explanation; and he attacks Paul because in seeking to *explain* Jesus' death, Paul undermines the nobility of Jesus' life. Nietzsche writes, 'There is no means of becoming a son of God except *by following the way of life taught by Christ*' (*WP* 170). He claims that Paul reverses and negates this teaching of 'salvation through faith', transforming it 'into the faith that one is to believe in some sort of miracu-lous subtraction of sins, accomplished not through man but through Christ's deed' (*WP* 170). Paul intellectualized the meaning of Jesus' death and reinterpreted it in abstract terms as a promise of redemption beyond life itself. As a conse-quence, Nietzsche asserts that Paul barred the possibility of relationship with the *living*. With Paul, Jesus no longer sym-bolizes the richness and singularity of life; he becomes a mere abstract motif of a means to an end, an end that is sought outside life (in the *death* of Christ). Jesus' life is subsequently undermined and loses its capacity to inspire our imitation. Nietzsche despises the Pauline Christ because he thinks it for-feits the immediacy of our human experience and replaces it with formal dogma.

Nietzsche often places the figures of Jesus and Paul – and Jesus and the Pauline Christ – in opposition. While Nietzsche claims that Jesus lived and practised a singular life without re-course to laws, explanations and theories, he contends that Paul, by contrast, was compelled to establish and consult laws that are abstract and universal. Nietzsche not only takes issue with Paul's move to universal values (which inevitably forfeits the richness of individual experience) but also with the particular content of these values. Paul's values are those of the weak and degenerate slave, so that in these values we find the 'symbolic transformed into crudities'. Nietzsche says, for instance, that in Paul 'resurrection' or 'rebirth' (which, for Nietzsche, comprises self-transcendence *within* the continual flux of life in the here and now) is 'understood as entry *into* "real life" . . . an historic eventuality which takes place some time or other after death'. Likewise, the noble value of 'brotherhood on the basis of sharing food and drink together after the Hebrew-Arabic custom' is transformed into 'the miracle of transubstantiation' (*WP* 170).

According to Nietzsche, Paul's *ressentiment* originates in his desire to seek revenge on the law – that which Paul perceives as the source of his failure and impotence. But Paul's *ressentiment* does not remain a *personal* issue – his sickness quickly spreads, giving rise to a pandemic of slave morality:

> What he [Paul] divined was that with the aid of a little sectarian movement on the edge of Judaism one could ignite a world conflagration; that with the symbol 'God on the Cross' one could sum up everything down-trodden, everything in secret revolt, the entire heritage of anarchistic agitation in the Empire into a tremendous power. (*AC* 58)

Paul: Nietzsche's scapegoat?

Nietzsche's treatment of Paul is severe, and scholars of Nietzsche tend to think he was unjustifiably harsh. Indeed, some suggest that he uses Paul as a scapegoat for his own views of the early Christian community in general. Several reasons for this are given. For instance, Nietzsche has been criticized for portraying Paul as the *decisive* figure in the creation of Christianity, rather than a key figure. Yet some scholars have also claimed that it is not Nietzsche who overestimates Paul's significance, but those commentators of Nietzsche who misread him as doing so. Thus, Tim Murphy draws our attention to the overlooked differentiation Nietzsche makes between ideas attributed to the early Christian community led by Peter and those attributed to Paul. (Murphy notes, for instance, that in *AC* 44 Nietzsche differentiates explicitly between the corrupted teachings of Peter and Paul. Similarly, in a list of biblical passages cited by Nietzsche in order to exemplify slavish Christian values (*AC* 45), out of the 13 that are cited from the New Testament, 10 are from the Synoptic Gospels and just 3 are from Paul.) Murphy concludes that it is more appropriate to regard Paul as a metaphorical figure (of *ressentiment*) for Nietzsche; and, as such, Paul is metaphorically synonymous with other religious figures (of *ressentiment*), such as Luther (whom Nietzsche alludes to as 'the second Paul' on the basis that Paul's failure to fulfil the law is matched with Luther's failure as a monk).

Another, more speculative, reason why Nietzsche might want to use Paul as a scapegoat is Jacob Taubes' suggestion that he was in fact very envious of Paul – for Paul succeeded in his realization of what Nietzsche himself sought: that is, a 'transvaluation of values'.[3] Thus, Paul managed to overturn those values he saw as corrupt and install in their place values made in his own image. In this respect Paul fulfilled Nietzsche's own project (but, of course, Paul's created values were not made in Nietzsche's own image, but in one of severe contrast).

Nietzsche's interpretation of Paul is certainly one-sided, and this can be attributed to a variety of psychological speculations. It is clear that more orthodox readings of Paul do not fit comfortably with Nietzsche's portrayal of him. For instance, Paul's propensity for affirming life and the 'Yes-saying instinct', which is an instinctual disposition celebrated by Nietzsche as integral to his own vision of life-affirmation, is, strangely, unacknowledged. Thus, Paul writes,

> For the Son of God, Jesus Christ, whom we proclaimed among you, Silvanus and Timothy and I, was not 'Yes and No'; but in

him it is always 'Yes.' For in him every one of God's promises
is a 'Yes.'   (2 Corinthians 1.19–20)

Just as Nietzsche claims that Paul turns Christ into a 'mere motif',
which he interprets as an emblem of Paul's own *ressentiment*
and hunger for power, we might want to claim that Nietzsche
similarly turns Paul into a motif, using him as a scapegoat
to discredit the central claims of Christianity. The Nietzsche
scholar Bruce Ellis Benson makes this point, suggesting that
Nietzsche uses Paul in the same way he claims Paul uses
Christ. In this sense, both Nietzsche and Paul are manipulating
values to their own personal ends, as expressions of their own
wills to power. Such similarity between Nietzsche's Paul and
Nietzsche himself suggests the former is a likely projection
of the latter. We could even go further in our psychological
speculation and suggest that Nietzsche's Paul is a product of
Nietzsche's own *ressentiment*: a scapegoat for the negative
feelings Nietzsche held towards his own Christian upbringing.
In such a scenario we would expect, as a matter of course,
Nietzsche's outward denigration of Paul to be somewhat
exaggerated.

In this chapter we have outlined Nietzsche's attack on Christianity for denigrating life as a source of meaning and value.
In the next chapter we shall turn our attention to Nietzsche's
famous and often misrepresented dictum, 'the death of God'.
We shall see how the death of God is a prerequisite for the
affirmation of a proper faith in life.

2

The death of God

The expression 'The death of God' is an obvious target for misappropriation and controversy. It has become a slogan that encompasses a variety of meanings. This is aptly demonstrated in the amusing twist of the term, which has God proclaim 'Nietzsche is dead!' This motto appears on many a commercial item (such as t-shirts, mugs and car-bumper stickers), and although it succeeds (arguably) in its witty intention, it also reveals in its simple inversion of the positions of Nietzsche and God a common misunderstanding of Nietzsche's term. By proclaiming the death of God, Nietzsche did not refer simply to the physical death of an ultimate and supposedly immortal 'being', analogous to his own inevitable mortal death. We shall see in this chapter that the death of God connotes for Nietzsche much more than this. As is the case with most concepts in Nietzsche's philosophy, the death of God does not have one definitive meaning, but several. We shall therefore outline the common explanations in Nietzschean scholarship of what or who died under the name of 'God', how it happened, why, and the implications of it for us and for religion in general.

Before we do so, it is important to bear in mind that although Nietzsche is most often associated with the death of God, he was not the first to proclaim it. In the early nineteenth century, a few decades before Nietzsche pronounced it, the concept of God's death was already associated with the loss of faith against the backdrop of the eighteenth-century European Enlightenment, most notably in the thought of the German philosophers G. W. F. Hegel (whom Nietzsche openly reviled) and Max Stirner (under his pseudonym Johann Kaspar Schmidt).

Nietzsche does not describe the death of God in detail, which means any attempt to explain it is problematic. Neither did he openly advocate previous accounts of the death of God, which might have shed light on his intended meaning. We are left simply with a handful of allusions to God's death in his works, predominantly in *The Gay Science* (1882) and *Thus Spoke Zarathustra* (1883–5). This fairly scant evidence has not, however, prevented scholars of Nietzsche from propounding their own ideas of what he meant by it, and who this dead God is. Indeed, it is generally agreed that when Nietzsche alludes to the death of God he refers either to the transcendent God of *metaphysics* or to the God of *compassion*.

Although commentators on Nietzsche may emphasize one of these aspects as Nietzsche's primary concern, it is not so easy to consider one without the other. For instance, in the previous chapter we saw that belief in metaphysical values is, for Nietzsche, a symptom of a weak disposition, one that approaches life from the perspective of will to truth rather than will to power. Just as there is no single facet to the identity of the dead God, there are a variety of ways in which God dies. On this, Nietzsche's Zarathustra is explicit. He tells us, 'when gods die, they always die many kinds of death'; and in Nietzsche's allusions to the death of God we find connotations of murder, suicide, abandonment and sacrifice.

Let us now turn to some of those passages that allude to the death of God, to see how God's nature – as metaphysical being or value, and as compassion – contribute to his death.

Death of the transcendent, metaphysical God

Perhaps the most celebrated passage to declare the death of God is Nietzsche's aphorism (as defined on page xv of the Introduction), 'The Madman' (*GS* 125). This is how it begins.

Have you heard of that madman who lit a lantern in the bright morning hours, ran to the market place, and cried incessantly: 'I seek God! I seek God!' – As many of those who did not believe in God were standing around just then, he provoked much laughter. Has he got lost? asked one. Did he lose his way like a child? asked another. Or is he hiding? Is he afraid of us? Has he gone on a voyage? emigrated? – Thus they yelled and laughed.

The madman jumped into their midst and pierced them with his eyes. 'Whither is God?' he cried: 'I will tell you. *We have killed him* – you and I.'

'All of us are his murderers. But how did we do this? How could we drink up the sea? Who gave us the sponge to wipe away the entire horizon? What were we doing when we un-chained this earth from its sun? Whither is it moving now? Whither are we moving? Away from all suns? Are we not plung-ing continually? Backward, sideward, forward, in all directions? Is there still any up or down? Are we not straying as through an infinite nothing? Do we not feel the breath of empty space? Has it not become colder? Is not night continually closing in on us? Do we not need light lanterns in the morning? Do we hear nothing as yet of the noise of gravediggers who are bury-ing God? Do we smell nothing as yet of the divine decom-position? Gods, too, decompose. God is dead. God remains dead. And we have killed him.'

This passage illustrates two principal ways in which commen-tators on Nietzsche have tended to conceptualize the tran-scendent God of metaphysics. The first is transcendence as ultimate *being* or entity (as insinuated in the witty phrase that has God proclaim Nietzsche's death); the second is tran-scendence as the impersonal, highest principle that makes all things possible and meaningful. In this passage we find the first position advocated by the group of people who refer to God as if he were an absent-minded person; and we find the second upheld by the madman, who regards God as the stabilizing foundation of meaning.

Both conceptions of the metaphysical God are apparent in Nietzsche's writings, and both attract their fair share of common misunderstandings, which lead to improbable and problematic interpretations of the death of God. For instance, as we shall see later in this chapter, some theologians have presumed incorrectly that Nietzsche killed off the impersonal God as transcendent highest principle in order to make room for a more authentic Christian conception of God: that is, one capable of personal relationship. Similarly, scholars often erroneously equate the death of God with God's non-existence: an equation that Nietzsche himself rejects outright (and notably, one endorsed by the ignorant people in the market place, who use it to ridicule and taunt the madman).

Let us now examine some of the more common explanations for the death of the transcendent God. We shall look first at the death of God as highest principle, where the widely held idea is that God died as a result of a gradual process of demystification, when rational values come to replace those of metaphysics. After this we shall outline the popular idea that God's death marks the end of his existence.

A slow, drawn-out death

Nietzsche suggests that God's death is a gradual event insofar as we, as finite beings, are able to perceive it. That is to say, although Nietzsche claims that 'God is dead, God remains dead', we fail either to realize or accept it, and as a consequence we continue to entertain the delusion that God is very much alive. Thus, at the end of the passage opposite (*GS* 125), Nietzsche refers to this lingering sense of God as a 'divine decomposition' that the majority of us are unable to smell. The madman further adds,

> 'I have come too early' . . . '[M]y time is not yet. This tremendous event is still on its way, still wandering; it has not yet reached the ears of men. Lightening and thunder require time; the light of stars requires time; deeds, though done, still require time to be seen and heard. This deed is still more distant from them than the most distant stars – *and yet they have done it themselves.*'

In the remaining two passages of *The Gay Science* that allude explicitly to the death of God, this divine remnant takes the form of a shadow. In section 108, entitled 'New Struggles', Nietzsche states,

> God is dead; but given the way of men, there may still be caves
> for thousands of years in which his shadow will be shown. –
> And we – we still have to vanquish his shadow.

Here the lingering shadow is a divine surplus that needs to be eradicated. Plato used an analogy of a cave to argue that we, as human beings, are able only to experience the shadows of the divine Forms of metaphysical truth. In this passage of Nietzsche, we find that the metaphysical form of God continues to cast its shadow even after God's death. In other words, we continue to delude ourselves into believing God is alive because such belief satisfies our degenerate needs and our will to truth. In Plato's analogy, humankind is imprisoned in its own world, unable to experience the light or true 'enlightenment' of the world beyond. By contrast, Nietzsche contends, enlightenment is found only in our world, and yet we shall remain like prisoners so long as we continue to create the need for a more perfect world and form beyond our grasp.

In a later passage of *GS* (343), the shadow is no longer lingering and unwanted; on the contrary, it is elusive and very much sought after. Here the shadow connotes full realization and acceptance of God's death. However, in this passage we are told that we are not yet able to perceive the shadow of the dead God and, consequently, we have not felt the repercussions of it:

> The greatest recent event – that 'God is dead,' that the belief in
> the Christian God has become unbelievable – is already start-
> ing to cast its first shadows over Europe. For the few at least,
> whose eyes – the *suspicion* in whose eyes is strong and subtle
> enough for this spectacle, some sun seems to have set and some
> ancient and profound trust has been turned into doubt; to them
> our old world must appear daily more like evening, more mis-
> trustful, stranger, 'older.' But in the main one must say: The event

itself is far too great, too distant, too remote from the multi-tude's capacity for comprehension even for the tidings of it to be thought of as having *arrived* as yet. Much less may one suppose that many people know as yet *what* this event really means – and how much must collapse now that this faith has been undermined because it was built upon this faith, propped up by it, grown into it; for example, the whole of our European morality.

Even we born guessers of riddles . . . we firstlings and pre-mature births of the coming century to whom the shadows that must soon envelop Europe really *should* have appeared by now . . .

Walter Kaufmann, the eminent translator and Nietzsche scholar, claims the clause at the beginning of this passage – that the belief in the Christian God has become unbelievable – 'is clearly offered as an explanation of "God is dead"'.[1] That is to say, Kaufmann thinks that Nietzsche's God died as soon as God became impossible to believe. And this interpretation has become an established explanation for Nietzsche's conception of the death of God.

The death of God is often regarded as a symbol for the rational age of secularization: an age in which the metaphysical 'horizon' is 'wiped away' because it is judged incoherent. The death of God in this respect is a gradual historical and cultural event (or lingering 'twilight') that took place in nineteenth-century Europe. It heralds the new era of modernity and industrialization in the wake of the rational Enlightenment of the previous century. In this sense Nietzsche was not responsible for the death of God (his genius lay, rather, in predicting the repercussions of the event for us, which we shall outline below). '*We have killed him*' the non-rational madman proclaims. The 'we' here refers to every thinker who helped to reformulate and reduce God and religious experience to rational terms, and who contributed more generally to the cultivation of the rational climate of the time. Thus, God died at the hands of a whole gang of people, whose notable members include, among others, the philosopher Immanuel Kant (who incorporated God within his elaborate epistemological system as an analogical image of systematic unity), Ludwig Feuerbach (who argued – like Nietzsche – that God is a mere projection of human need) and David Strauss (who argued for mythical interpretations of Jesus' life and miracles).

Although the death of God may be symbolized by the cultural shift in conditions of belief that made God incoherent and unbelievable, Nietzsche made efforts to show that God's death is not a matter for rational reflection. That is to say, although our rational belief-system does not allow God to live, this does not mean we have rational *proof* that God cannot live and does not live for those people whose belief-systems incorporate non-reason. Indeed, the death of God is proclaimed by a madman: it is he alone – the one who embodies the opposite of reason – who is aware of the full force and meaning of God's death. By contrast, the crowd in the market place, who represent the rational mindset of the day, fail to engage with the meaning of God's death. They regard God's death from the perspective of comfortable reason only – as a formula or prescription of God's non-existence – and cannot experience the terrifying implications of it for their lives. These 'onlookers' to the madman are onlookers in life; they regard God's death as old news and mock the madman for his concern.

Nietzsche's account of the market place meeting between madman and disbelieving onlookers is thought to echo deliberately the New Testament narratives where Jesus proclaims his revelatory news to the disbelieving Pharisees and Sadducees. Thus, the madman's words, 'My time is not yet', echo those of Jesus, 'My time has not yet come' (John 7.6; cf. 2.4). Nietzsche's madman, like Jesus before him, is a prophet who stands outside the spirit of his time in order to herald the coming of the new. We could also say the same for Nietzsche himself, who experienced life on the edge of society and who failed to impress his contemporaries with his portents of the rise of secularization. Indeed, in the last ten years of his life, Nietzsche physically embodied the madman, apparently believing himself in his deranged state to be the personified Christ.

Murder versus atheism: death of God versus God's non-existence

In the previous chapter we saw Nietzsche criticize the will to truth as a delusional approach to life, one that made life appear more comfortable to those who were unable to affirm its chaotic flux. God, as a manifestation of will to truth, was considered a mere projection of human weakness. In this chapter, we find this God-delusion dispelled by the rigors of the prevailing rational mindset. But this does not mean that reason can overcome the will to truth and operate from the position of will to power. Far from it. The will to truth does not come to an end when one of its principal outlets or manifestations does; it lingers on, forging other ways to express itself. The rational, scientific outlook is simply one of these new manifestations of the will to truth: a straightforward exchange for God. Thus, Nietzsche claims, 'it is still a *metaphysical faith* upon which our faith in science rests ... [W]e godless antimetaphysicians still take our fire, too, from the flame [of] Christian faith' (*GS* 344). The onlookers in the market place simply depend on a different crutch from Christians. When they purport to know that God does not exist, they are not speaking from a more advanced perspective than that of the madman who searches for God in vain. On the contrary, because Nietzsche maintains that to settle on the truth is to be deluded, we may assume that the madman is in fact closer to the truth because he has yet to find its source.

Nietzsche is not concerned with questions of God's existence; to be so is to adopt the will to truth. Nietzsche would rather remove all crutches and delusions of will to truth, and affirm life through the will to power. He writes,

> In former times, one sought to prove that there is no God – today one indicates how the belief that there is a God could *arise* and how this belief acquired its weight and importance: a counter-proof that there is no God thereby becomes superfluous. – When in former times one had refuted the 'proofs of the existence of God' put forward, there always remained the

doubt whether better proofs might not be adduced than those just refuted: in those days atheists did not know how to make a clean sweep. (*D* 95)

Hitherto one has always attacked Christianity not merely in a modest way but in the wrong way . . . The question of the mere 'truth' of Christianity – whether in regard to the existence of God or to the legendary history of origin . . . is quite beside the point. (*AC* 47)

Thus, Nietzsche's attack against Christianity is more profound and sweeping than the more conventional approach that questions God's existence, for he maintains that even if God were to exist, God is too despicable a being to warrant our attention, let alone our worship or dedication. God is dead not because he does not exist, but because he is unworthy of his divinity.

What sets us apart is not that we recognize no God, either in history or in nature or behind nature – but that we find that which has been reverenced as God not 'godlike' but pitiable, absurd, harmful, not merely an error but a crime against life. We deny God as God. [I]f this God of the Christians were proved to us to exist, we should know even less how to believe in him. (*AC* 162–3)

The death of God is a matter of taste or instinct. In a statement that seems at odds with the idea that God's death is a gradual event of rational demystification, Nietzsche writes, 'I have absolutely no knowledge of atheism as an outcome of reasoning, still less as an event: with me it is obvious by instinct' (*EH* 21).

Nietzsche is keen to distance God's death from God's non-existence, and instinctual 'murder' from reasoned atheism. These contrasting positions are represented respectively by the madman – who proclaims, '*We have killed him*' – and his resistant audience, the 'non-believers'. Nietzsche wants his nineteenth-century readers to recognize themselves as murderers rather than passive atheists. He wants us to take responsibility for the value of our own lives and for realizing our human possibility. This is done, he argues, by destroying the crutches that inhibit our imagination and our risk-taking. He laments at the failure of so many of us, mere 'onlookers', who are not ready to accept our role as murderers of God, believing it 'madness'; who attribute God's death to the gradual advance of reason and science. To shirk off responsibility for our being is a sign of degeneracy; and the person who understands his or her atheism as a matter of rational deduction is as weak minded as the Christian who believes in God.

Non-rational death: beyond rational enlightenment

The idea that God's death is for Nietzsche simply an inevitable event or result of rational enlightenment is dubious. The Nietzsche commentator Giles Fraser argues against the validity of this conception, claiming Nietzsche's philosophy to be outside the Enlightenment tradition. Fraser argues that the death of God is not the culmination of a rational process 'which reduced God to a certain sort of metaphysics (a tradition which then went on to dispose of metaphysics, thus finishing God off in the process)'. Fraser finds Nietzsche more realistically placed within the Renaissance tradition, and 'far more an inheritor of the scepticism of the ancients than a spokesman for a society which finds the idea of God "no longer conceivable"'.[2] The principal reason why commentators on Nietzsche misconstrue him in this way is, Fraser maintains, because they are heavily influenced by a distorted interpretation proffered by the philosopher Martin Heidegger.

Heidegger was one of the most influential philosophers of the twentieth century, whose work was principally concerned with the question of being. It is generally thought that Heidegger appropriated Nietzsche's thought to his own ends, branding Nietzsche a 'metaphysical thinker' in the process. More specifically, Heidegger described Nietzsche as 'the last metaphysical thinker'. This is because he saw Nietzsche as having opened the way for what subsequently became known as postmodern philosophy (in which all metanarratives – such as God as ultimate meaning – had dissolved); and yet, significantly, he regarded Nietzsche's own philosophy as trapped within the metaphysical thinking he sought to eliminate. According to Heidegger, the attempt to overcome metaphysics that he saw in Nietzsche's death of God is inextricably tied to metaphysics. Such an attempt, Heidegger says, is 'a mere countermovement' to metaphysics, which 'necessarily remains, as does everything "anti", held fast in the essence of that over against which it moves'.[3] In this sense, the God of metaphysics does not die through the instigation of an opposing ideal. (In Nietzsche's terms, we can describe this futile attempt to overcome metaphysics as a reinforcement of the will to truth, where the underlying *shadow* of the will to truth is sustained, and only its manifest expression changes.)

If we resituate Nietzsche within a different intellectual tradition (for instance, from Enlightenment to Renaissance, as Fraser would), then our interpretation of his thought will inevitably change. However, such a task is very difficult to do, not least because Nietzsche's many perspectives seek to evade categorization. (Furthermore, the boundaries between such categories as Renaissance and Enlightenment are themselves contentious.) Nevertheless, Fraser contends that Nietzsche is attempting to do something fundamentally different from that which Heidegger recognizes. That is to say, Nietzsche does not seek to get rid of God by trying to eradicate the metaphysical foundations upon which God depends; he is, rather, rejecting God on the grounds of God's utility and worth.

Nietzsche's writings portray contrasting conceptions in the way God and God's death are valued. We have so far described how Nietzsche construes the death of God as a passive outcome of the competition between reason and metaphysics as opposing epistemological systems (both of which are grounded within the will to truth). Shortly, we shall turn our attention to the fundamentally different approach alluded to above, whereby Nietzsche portrays God's death as a result of his corrupt and degenerate values of compassion. But before we do so, let us briefly return to the previous conception, so as not to pass by the potentially exciting idea that we have only touched on: that Nietzsche's metaphysical God cannot die, or that God still, somehow, remains in Nietzsche's thought.

Death of the transcendent God: good news for Christianity?

At first sight, the notion that God may still remain in Nietzsche's thought is theologically exciting. Indeed, some theological thinkers have taken it upon themselves to locate and unearth this hidden God – a Christian God even – from the depths of Nietzsche's writing. However, upon closer inspection any excitement we may have had is quickly dispelled, as their attempts to resurrect the Christian God prove problematic. Certainly, the extent of Nietzsche's obsession with God suggests he is unable and unwilling to let God go completely (a point argued both by Lou Andreas-Salomé, Nietzsche's close friend and disenchanted love-interest, and C. G. Jung, who diagnosed Nietzsche's personality through an examination of *Thus Spoke Zarathustra*). But several commentators on Nietzsche attempt to go a step further and understand the death of the metaphysical and transcendent God as necessary if God is to become manifest in a more authentic and appropriate Christian form. These thinkers believe, contra Heidegger, that the metaphysical God can and indeed did die and, moreover, that God's death is at the heart of the Christian message.

For instance, the theologian Eberhard Jüngel believes Nietzsche killed off a distorted version of the genuine Christian God. By proclaiming the transcendent God dead, Jüngel finds Nietzsche's God free from the restriction of total self-sufficiency and subsequently able to sustain personal relationship with humanity.[4] Another instance is the controversial theologian Thomas J. J. Altizer, who helped found the 1960s radical Death of God movement, which incorporated the thought of Nietzsche (whom Altizer called a 'radical Christian'). Altizer argues that the transcendent aspect of God dies when God is reborn in the person of Christ. God's incarnation in Christ is a permanent self-emptying (*kenosis*) in which God negates or annihilates himself. The death of God therefore overrides the distance that previously separated God from humanity, and subsequently removes the possibility of sin (which literally means separation from God).[5]

These instances are similar in principle to the idea that Nietzsche favours Jesus, the representative of life, over Christ the representative of death – an idea we explored in the previous chapter. From a Christian perspective, we find in Nietzsche the personal God privileged over the God of transcendence, on the basis that the former encourages human connection while the latter enforces its separation. However, Nietzsche would not endorse these Christian arguments. Thus, just as Nietzsche's assault on Christ *does not* make room for discipleship of Jesus, Nietzsche does not get rid of the transcendent God in order that we might be better off in connection and personal relationship with God. Similarly, although Nietzsche finds Jesus preferable to Christ, he still regards Jesus as weak and naïve (something we shall discuss in more detail at the end of the next chapter). Likewise, as we shall see shortly, Nietzsche abhors the kind of personal relationship Christianity extols.

The personal and compassionate God is the second common candidate for Nietzsche's dead God. Nietzsche's account of the death of this God makes futile those attempts to resurrect the Christian God within Nietzsche. Let us now turn to this account to determine how God's compassionate nature is thought by Nietzsche to lead to God's death.

Death of the Crucified: God of compassion

Nietzsche's attack on Christianity is principally an attack on its corrupt and corrupting values; and metaphysics and compassion are singled out as the primary agents of the fraudulent Christian enterprise.

Commentators on Nietzsche often highlight compassion as the more devastating value of the two. Indeed, as we saw in the previous chapter, Nietzsche makes it clear in *AC* that the greatest perpetrator of theological corruption was not the metaphysician Plato (or St Thomas Aquinas), but St Paul, whom Nietzsche castigated for inventing the crucified God who sacrificed himself for his love for humanity. Indeed, we might argue that compassion (rather than transcendence) is what makes God distinctively Christian. Thus, Nietzsche's attack on Christianity inevitably attempts to undermine the compassionate nature of God.

Unlike the transcendent God, which is completely indifferent to its adherents, the God of compassion enters into personal relationship with his disciples and engages with their human suffering. The God of compassion affirms the coward's position more directly and affectively. But this does not mean the transcendent God of metaphysics does not also affirm cowardice. Indeed, the two aspects of God work together to spread their debilitating infection. The coward enjoys a special and immediate relationship with the God of compassion; and to call this God transcendent is to universalize 'compassion', making it a metaphysical value true for all time, all places, and for all people.

Whereas the transcendent God dies an impersonal and premeditated death (at the hands of rational conspirators, who work together to substantiate the rational grounds that can no longer support God's existence), the compassionate God dies a personal death, provoked by the souring of his relationship with humanity. Let us now turn to *TSZ*, the book that immediately follows *GS*, to find allusion to the death of the personal God of compassion. (It should be noted that just as both accounts of God and his death can be discerned in *GS*, they are also found in *TSZ*.)

TSZ is a philosophical work of fiction, occasionally poetic in style, and rich in metaphor and ambiguity (something that is aptly expressed in its subtitle: *A book for everyone and no one*). There are several passages in *TSZ* that allude explicitly to the death of God or to the dead God, and yet the emphasis of *TSZ* is rather on the implications of his death, as envisioned through the eyes of its main character, Zarathustra. We shall outline some of these implications at the end of this chapter and explore them in greater depth in the chapters that follow. But for now, let us first determine who Zarathustra is, and see what he has to say about the death of God.

Who is Zarathustra?

As with all ideas in Nietzsche's work, Zarathustra's identity is not easily deduced. There are a variety of interpretations, including the idea that Zarathustra is a dramatized version of Nietzsche himself.

Historically, Zarathustra, or Zoroaster, was a Persian prophet who founded Zoroastrianism (the religion of the Sassanid Empire of Persia). It is unclear when he lived, and indeed if he ever did, though scholars have argued for a date at the beginning of the sixth century BC, and others, who maintain that Zarathustra is the author of the *Gâthâ's* (a part of the *Avesta*, the holy book of Zoroastrianism), place him as early as the fourteenth or thirteenth century BC.

Zoroastrianism took a dualistic approach to life, defining human existence as a struggle between the opposites of 'truth' and 'lie' and their respective personifications in Ahura Mazda (God, or 'the Better') and Ahriman (the Devil, or 'the Bad'). Zoroastrianism helped to shape the slavish morality of the Christian tradition that Nietzsche sought to destroy, and yet Nietzsche's Zarathustra stands in complete contrast to this historic figure of Zoroastrianism. Nietzsche portrays a new and radically different Zarathustra, one who turns traditional Christian morality on its head in order to dissolve the dichotomy of good and evil.

In his own words, and speaking as 'the first immoralist', Nietzsche tells us that his version of Zarathustra embodies 'the opposite' of 'what constitutes the tremendous historical uniqueness of that [original] Persian'.

> Zarathustra was the first to consider in the struggle between good and evil the actual wheel in the working of things: the translation of morality into the realm of metaphysics, as force,

cause, end-in-itself, is *his* work . . . Zarathustra *created* this most fateful of errors, morality: consequently he must also be the first to *recognize* it . . . His teaching, and his alone, upholds truthfulness as the supreme virtue – that is to say, the opposite of the *cowardice* of the 'idealist', who takes flight in face of reality . . . Have I been understood? – the self-overcoming of morality through truthfulness, the self-overcoming of the moralist into his opposite – *into me* – that is what the name Zarathustra means in my mouth.

(EH, 'Why I am a destiny' 3)

Nietzsche's Zarathustra is opposed to Christianity. Just as the historical Zarathustra helped shape Christianity, Nietzsche's Zarathustra has returned in order to correct his mistake, and radically to reconfigure his invention. Because Christianity is no longer in touch with the world, Zarathustra must be reborn; he must come back to show that God is dead and to eradicate the inherent difference between 'good' and 'evil'. In *TSZ* we follow him on his mission to preach the revaluation of values – of going beyond good and evil. And central to his teaching is the death of the defunct God and destruction of the old law tablets. Zarathustra has come to unravel Christianity, and in a wonderfully ironic move Nietzsche adopts a biblical style of narrative in order to convey Zarathustra's message. *TSZ* is rife with biblical allusion. Perhaps the most notable parallel is in the figure of Zarathustra himself, who closely parallels Jesus in character, teaching, and in the people and events he encounters during his ministry. Nietzsche plays ironically on their similarity throughout. For instance, while both figures proclaim the 'glad tidings' of the coming of a new kingdom here on earth and within us all, for Zarathustra its arrival is premised on the death of God.

Let us now turn to some of those passages in *TSZ* that allude to the death of the compassionate God. They will reveal personal motivations for God's death, including the need for God himself to escape his overwhelming compassion for humankind, and also human revenge for the ugliness God bestowed upon humanity.

A pitiful death: suicide and avenged murder

Perhaps the most interesting references to the death of God in *TSZ* are those that present it as an outcome of the relationship he himself had established with the human race. In other words, God's death is regarded as a consequence of the anti-life conditions he instilled in his relationship with humankind, conditions that exalt death and corruption.

This is exemplified by God's desire for pity, which for Nietzsche is a degenerate value promoted by slave morality. Pity is a sickness 'that makes suffering contagious' (*AC* 7); 'a weakness, like every losing of oneself through a *harmful* affect. It *increases* the amount of suffering in the world' (*D* 134). According to Nietzsche, the enslaved Jewish people refashioned their God as an embodiment and valorization of such slavish values as pity and compassion. Through Zarathustra, we learn that God, in his infinite compassion, is so overwhelmed by pity for mankind that it kills him. Nietzsche tells us that God 'loses himself' through the 'harmful affect' of pity, which is to say that the impulse of pity has become master of God and subsequently determines his very being. In this respect God dies as a result of his own defective nature – of the harmful value he is both seized by and has come to embody. God therefore creates the conditions for his own death and, in this sense, his death can be likened to suicide.

Thus, as the epigraph to Part Four of *TSZ*, and in the section 'Of the compassionate' of Part Two, Zarathustra proclaims:

> Alas, where in the world have there been greater follies than with the compassionate? And what in the world has caused more suffering than the follies of the compassionate? Woe to all lovers who cannot surmount pity! Thus spoke the Devil to me once: 'Even God has his Hell: it is his love for man. And I lately heard him say these words: 'God is dead; God has died of his pity for man.'

Similarly, in the section 'Retired from service' Zarathustra converses with the last Christian pope, and about his dead God, Zarathustra asks:

'Do you know *how* he died? Is it true what they say, that pity choked him, that he saw how *man* hung on the Cross and could not endure it, that love for man became his Hell and at last his death?' The old pope, however, did not answer, but looked away shyly and with a pained and gloomy expression.

Eventually, however, the retired pope does respond:

'[A]t length he grew old and soft and mellow and compassionate, more like a grandfather than a father, most like a tottery old grandmother. Then he sat, shrivelled, in his chimney corner, fretting over his weak legs, world-weary, weary of willing, and one day suffocated through his excessive pity.'

Pity is again portrayed as the reason for God's death in Zarathustra's conversation with 'the ugliest man', whom Zarathustra encounters shortly after he takes leave of the retired pope. This time, however, the nature of God's death is explained as murderous revenge at the hands of the 'ugliest man'. The ugliest man tells Zarathustra he murdered God because he could no longer bear the unrelenting pity of God, which had penetrated deep into the ugliness of the man's very being. We learn that ugliness in itself is not a problem for the ugliest man (indeed, he actually reveres his ugliness); what is problematic and intolerable is the common response and effect his ugliness often has on others, namely pity. Pity drew unwanted attention to his ugliness, redefining it as something impoverished, inferior and dishonourable. Pity had become an inevitable response to ugliness under the reign of God, such that the ugliest man felt tainted to his very core.

This section of *TSZ*, 'The ugliest man', describes how Zarathustra entered a valley of death, whereupon he came across a creature 'shaped like a man and yet hardly a man, something unutterable'. At the sight of so despicable and ugly a figure, Zarathustra blushes in great shame and turns away in order to take his leave. At this point the creature asks Zarathustra to solve the riddle of his identity, and in response Zarathustra is overwhelmed with pity before he correctly answers, 'I know you well . . . *You are the murderer of God!*'

Although Zarathustra experiences immense pity, he also feels great shame at the sight of the ugliest man; and it is his shame that excites the ugliest man, who receives it as a great and rare honour. While Zarathustra was noble enough to respond to the ugly creature by turning away from him in shame, thereby acknowledging him for who or what he was, God, by contrast, simply stared an all-encompassing and penetrating stare, causing the ugliest man to question his own identity and nature. It was precisely because God could not look away in shame that the ugliest man felt compelled to murder him. The ugliest man says to Zarathustra,

> You warned against pity – no one else, only you and those of your kind. You are ashamed of the shame of the great sufferer . . . But, he [God] *had* to die: he looked with eyes that saw *everything* – he saw the depths and the abysses of man, all man's hidden disgrace and ugliness. His pity knew no shame: he crept into my dirtiest corners. This most curious, most over-importunate, over-compassionate god had to die. He always saw *me*: I desired to take revenge on such a witness – or cease to live myself. The god who saw everything, *even man*: this god had to die! Many could not *endure* that such a witness should live.

Pity, according to Nietzsche, increases suffering in several ways. For instance, it can incite feelings of inferiority within the person who is pitied, causing him or her to retaliate against the person who pities; and it can detract from the pain and suffering essential to his or her nobility and personal growth. Both are apparent with the ugliest man, who retaliated against the infinite pity of God and also seemed unable to revere himself so long as God continued to force 'help' upon him:

> [B]e it the pity of a god, be it human pity: pity is contrary to modesty. And unwillingness to help may be nobler than that virtue which comes running with help.

Although Zarathustra proclaims pity to be contrary to modesty this does not mean that immodesty is pitiful. Indeed, Nietzsche deems immodesty in its own right a noble and self-affirming value. Interestingly, Zarathustra tells us that God's arrogant declaration in front of all other gods, that he alone is the one true god, caused the other gods to die from laughter ('Of the apostates'). And if it weren't for the Christian God being otherwise so despicable in infecting humankind with a life-debilitating disease, Nietzsche or Zarathustra might have been more favourably disposed to God's lack of modesty. Zarathustra, however, is quick to quash God's noble self-promotion and any sense of achievement or fulfilment God may have derived from it, by making an arrogant declaration of his own: '*If there were gods, how could I endure not to be a god! Hence there are no gods*' ('On the blissful islands').

The remaining allusions to the death of God in *TSZ* are fleeting, and are generally enlisted by Zarathustra to support or highlight another aspect of his teaching. While the madman of *GS* has only just felt the full force of the death of God, Zarathustra considers it old news, and it is for this reason that his teaching looks beyond the death of God to the new, life-affirming values that can be cultivated only after God's death. These references tend to be of minor interest in themselves, but help to direct our attention beyond God's death to the consequences of it.

Postmortem: after God

The death of God signals the dissolution of a prescribed system of enforced order and meaning, and our immersion in the endless flux of life. This dissolution of meaning is called 'nihilism', wherein 'the highest values devalue themselves'. The 'aim is lacking' and ' "Why?" finds no answer' (*WP* 2).

We can respond to this nihilism either passively or actively. Passive nihilism is a pessimistic approach: one of despair and loss of energy and power, in which a person's will becomes stagnant and incapable of creative acts. Active nihilism, on the other hand, is an optimistic approach, and 'a sign of increased power'. Nietzsche's philosophy is grounded in this sense of optimism. In the previous chapter we saw how keen he is for us to respond to the horror of life's eternal flux with joyful affirmation. Likewise, we find Nietzsche regarding the sheer terror and anxiety of the madman's lamentations as cause for jubilation. Thus, in GS 343 there are phrases similar to those spoken in sorrow by the madman now expressed with joy; and as the title of this aphorism reveals, the madman's proclamation constitutes '*the meaning of our cheerfulness*'. The consequences of God's death are, Nietzsche says,

> [Q]uite the opposite of what one might perhaps expect: They are not at all sad and gloomy but rather like a new and scarcely describable kind of light, happiness, relief, exhilaration, encouragement, dawn.
>
> Indeed, we philosophers and 'free spirits' feel, when we hear the news that 'the old god is dead,' as if a new dawn shone on us; our heart overflows with gratitude, amazement, premonitions, expectation. At long last the horizon appears free to us again, even if it should not be bright: at long last our ships may venture out again, venture out to face any danger; all the daring of the lover of knowledge is permitted again: the sea, *our* sea, lies open again; perhaps there has never yet been such an 'open sea'. (*GS* 343)

Nihilism is an horrific proposition that can leave us paralysed. Life can be seen, as the madman sees it, as empty, purposeless and absurd. All values are exposed to us as the genealogy of our prejudices, so that truth is merely what we collectively desire to be true. And yet Nietzsche, with his prophet Zarathustra, rejoices in the freedom and the immense potential that nihilism can offer. They herald the emergence of new values, which will enable humanity to prosper, to act and to affirm the flux of life as meaningful. But what are these new values? How, asks the mad man,

> shall we comfort ourselves, the murderers of all murderers? What was holiest and mightiest of all that the world has yet owned has bled to death under our knives: who will wipe this blood off us? What water is there for us to clean ourselves? What festivals of atonement, what sacred games shall we have to invent? Is not the greatness of this deed too great for us? Must

we ourselves not become gods simply to appear worthy of it?
There has never been a greater deed; and whoever is born after
us – for the sake of this deed he will belong to a higher history
than all history hitherto.   (*GS* 125)

The remaining chapters in this book will go some way towards answering these questions, but the answers will not be
straightforward because the revaluation of values is not a set
of prescribed laws or values superimposed on to life to give
a deceptive order and structure. Rather, the revaluation of
values is a radical approach to life that develops from out of
our capacity to affirm the meaninglessness of life.

After the death of God we can approach life either passively,
in despair or in denial (unaware of the need for radical
change), or actively, as dynamic creators continually refashion-
ing our lives. Nietzsche's project argues for the latter. And his
idea of the death of God can be regarded as a test to see how
capable we are – individually and collectively – of upholding
this position, and not succumbing to passivity. It can thus be
construed as a test of our strength of will: to determine how
we fare when exposed to the abyss of meaninglessness without the safety net of delusory truth. (We shall discuss this
'test' further in Chapter 4, where it is described within the wider
context of Nietzsche's overall project and a case put for its
particular relevance to Christian practice today.)

The revaluation of values proposed by Nietzsche is a new
approach to life that proffers a new humanity and a new way
of being. Although the death of God leads to the nihilistic
erasure of structured meaning, this does not mean that all
values are made equal and 'anything goes'. Nietzsche wants to
establish a new hierarchy of value or 'order of rank' based
not on truth, but on strength of will or power. The death of
God is thus an occasion to be cheerful because it signals the
end of human equality that was instigated by slave morality.
Nietzsche's revaluation of values intends to separate strong
individuals, who exercise the will to power, from weaker ones,
who adopt the will to truth. Thus, Zarathustra proclaims,

> God has died. And let us not be equal before the mob. You Higher
> Men, depart from the market-place! . . . You Higher Men, this
> God was your greatest danger. Only since he has lain in the grave
> have you again been resurrected . . . God has died: now *we*
> desire – that the Superman shall live.   ('Of the Higher Man')

The death of God signals the death of slave culture and the
re-emergence of a higher culture – of what Nietzsche calls the
Übermensch (the superman). We shall explore the meaning of
the *Übermensch* in the following chapter. But for now we will
simply note that the *Übermensch* embodies the revaluation
of values, and the overcoming of Christianity. Whereas the
Christian puts his or her faith in the transcendent God of
compassion and the infinite world beyond our own, the
Übermensch puts his or her faith in the creative strife of the
here and now. Zarathustra proclaims,

> Once blasphemy against God was the greatest blasphemy,
> but God died, and thereupon these blasphemers died too. To
> blaspheme the earth is now the most dreadful offence, and
> to esteem the bowels of the Inscrutable more highly than the
> meaning of the earth.   (Prologue 3)

Zarathustra's new faith is expressed as 'a leaping circle dance
over every here and there and yonder', a dance that reflects the
flux of life and its eternal coming to be and passing away. The
death of God enables the eternal recurrence of living life in
the moment. Eternal life is found right here, in our world and
on our earth, and not outside time in a world infinitely beyond
our own.

In the chapter that follows we shall examine Nietzsche's
earth-bound faith through three of its principal and interdependent expressions: the chthonic god Dionysus, who represents the cycle of creation and destruction; what Nietzsche
calls the doctrine of 'eternal recurrence', which is heroically
affirmed by Dionysus; and the *Übermensch*, who is the antici-
pated man (or woman) who will adopt nothing short of a
Dionysian attitude to life.

3

Nietzsche's faith:
the revaluation of values

For Nietzsche, God is dead; but this does not signal the end to religion. In the previous chapter we saw that Nietzsche is not concerned about the existence or non-existence of God, but with the moral question of what constitutes divinity: of what kind of God is worthy of our attention and worship. Nietzsche attacks the Christian God because it is an ideal of the slavish, degenerate masses, of those people who use their God as an excuse for their own failure to engage with the demands of life.

So what kind of God is worthy of divinity and of our worship? For Nietzsche, the answer is a noble God, a God who affirms our humanity and the instability of life. Nietzsche invites us to conceive of this God. In a note of 1887–8 he writes:

> Let us remove supreme goodness from the concept of God: it is unworthy of a god. Let us also remove supreme wisdom: it is the vanity of philosophers that is to be blamed for this mad notion of God as a monster of wisdom: he had to be as like them as possible. No! God the *supreme power* – that suffices! Everything follows from it, 'the world' follows from it!
>
> (*WP* 534)

Nietzsche's noble God embodies the will to power, and the capacity continually to create, destroy and recreate values in parallel to the ebb and flow of life. At the end of the previous chapter we saw that Zarathustra has an earth-bound faith, which is celebrated or worshipped by a vivacious 'leaping circle dance'. Nietzsche's God thrives on earth. God is not worshipped as separate from life, but is life itself. Thus, when

Zarathustra asserts, 'I should believe only in a God who knows how to dance', we find his God identified with the very dance – or ebb and flow – of life.

According to Nietzsche, the Christian God is made manifest in the corrupt figure of Christ on earth, in order to redeem us from our sinful human nature. And to contrast with this unworthy divinity, Nietzsche conceives a noble divinity, one rooted to the earth and identifiable with the movement or dynamic of human creative endeavour and self-overcoming.

How can we move from the Christian ideal to that of Nietzsche? And what, exactly, does Nietzsche's ideal comprise? In previous chapters we have seen Nietzsche 'philosophize with a hammer' in order to destroy Christian structures of meaning: something that has left – as the madman laments – a nihilistic world devoid of absolute meaning. In this chapter, we shall see the various ways in which Nietzsche creates out of destruction and the enduring chaotic free-flow of life.

To help us on our way, Zarathustra offers a parable called 'Of the three metamorphoses' that describes the series of transformations that need to take place in order for us to progress spiritually from degenerate Christian to creative noble. Zarathustra symbolizes the three metamorphoses of spirit as camel, lion and child respectively. The spirit, he tells us, becomes a camel once it has conformed to the dictates of tradition. This animal symbolizes humanity laden down with 'the heaviest things': with guilt and sin given to it from the Christian moral interpretation of life. Only 'in the loneliest desert', where the spirit has space to self-reflect, can the second metamorphosis occur, thereby enabling the spirit to become a lion. The lion represents the autonomous person capable of pride and self-respect, courage and strength. To become a lion is to overcome – by sheer will – the weight of those moral imperatives, the 'Thou shalts' that had burdened the camel. The lion is a philosopher of the hammer; it instigates nihilism and *tabula rasa* to enable recreation. But the might of the lion cannot create new values for itself (it simply destroys those of others); hence a further transformation of spirit is required.

Echoing Matthew 18.3 ('unless you change and become like children, you will never enter the kingdom of heaven'), Zarathustra tells us the lion must become a child. The child symbolizes 'innocence and forgetfulness, a new beginning, a sport, a self-propelling wheel, a first motion, a sacred Yes'. The spirit as child, Zarathustra says, 'wills *its own* will' and 'wins *its own* world'.

Here we see that Nietzsche's faith is in the innocence of children and does not culminate in the 'blond beast' of the mighty lion, as is often supposed. However, this parable raises as many questions as it answers. For instance, how exactly can the lion become a child? The camel seems to become a lion through self-reflection and great effort of will, but it is difficult to imagine how a creature of war can become an innocent child, one completely unaware of all the battles that have gone on before.[1] We might also question the implication that spiritual excellence is achieved through a state of unconsciousness or lack of memory. Elsewhere in Nietzsche's writings, however, we find support for this somewhat bizarre idea. For instance, in a note of 1888 he writes, 'Only automatism makes possible perfection in life and creation' (*WP* 68); and elsewhere he asserts,

> The higher rationale of such a procedure lies in the intention of gradually making the way of life recognized as correct . . . unconscious: so that a complete automatism of instinct is achieved – the precondition for any kind of mastery, any kind of perfection in the art of living.　　　　　(*AC* 57)

This idea begins to make sense when we recall our discussion in Chapter 1 of the 'master', who is incapable of *ressentiment* because he does not have the capacity to reflect upon (and thus retain in memory) those misdeeds done to him. In this respect, the capacity for unconsciousness or ability to forget those aspects of life detrimental to one's creative development (such as slavish *ressentiment*) is extremely useful and spiritually rewarding.

Nietzsche's philosophy is not a system of doctrines on how to live life, but an evocation of faith in life: of becoming a child rather than being a worldly-wise adult. Likewise, the morality of his faith is not one that seeks to improve and reform according to an ideal; it is, rather, a morality that affirms what or who one is in the here and now. Just as the ugliest man revered his ugliness, Nietzsche wants us to find joy in our shortcomings and our strife, because it is part and parcel of who we are and the life we inevitably find ourselves within.

Nietzsche's faith is in the dynamics of self-surpassing, of coming-to-be. He cannot teach us what we have to do in order to surpass ourselves as this will mean different things to each of us, depending on our individual dispositions to life. The best Nietzsche can do is to express what self-surpassing means to him personally. He does not want us to emulate his formula and try to embody his own developing self, for this would mean we have not found our own selves and are not, therefore, disciples of his faith. This is illustrated by Zarathustra's pronouncement in Part One of *TSZ*: 'One repays a teacher badly, if one remains a pupil . . . Now do I bid you lose me and find yourselves; and only when you have denied me will I return unto you.' Similarly, in Part Three he contends, 'You have your way. I have my way. As for the right way, the correct way, and the only way, it does not exist.'

If we are to follow Nietzsche and make sense of his faith, we must abandon his teaching and engage with our own selves. It is to this end that his writing is convoluted and confusing to read. He offers symbols, parables and competing perspectives in order for us to take responsibility for our own interpretations (and perhaps even to make us so frustrated with trying to decipher his intentions that we throw his books on the floor and focus on the living of our lives, instead of using his ideas as objects of abstract reflection). In outlining Nietzsche's conception of self-surpassing we shall see what Nietzsche had hoped we would pay attention to, before 'usefully forgetting' in favour of our own creative formulas for living.

Up until now, we have glimpsed several allusions to Nietzsche's conception of self-surpassing, but now we shall outline three principal expressions of it noted at the end of

Chapter 2. These are the *Übermensch* (or 'superman' or 'over-human'), Dionysus and the 'eternal recurrence' (or 'eternal return of the same'). These notions embody Nietzsche's faith and are often interpreted as indicative of his commitment to the divine.

The Übermensch

The vagueness of Nietzsche's description of the *Übermensch* has led to a variety of explanations, some of which are fanciful and absurd. Perhaps the most notorious misrepresentation is the doctrine of the 'Master Race' expounded by the Nazis. Add to this Aryan 'blond beast' the all-American red-caped superhero and 'man of steel', 'Superman' from DC-comic-book fame (who shares his name with the unfortunate traditional English translation of *Übermensch*), and we lose sight of Nietzsche's important notion, which is too often hidden behind a ridiculous, distorted façade.

Fragmentary allusions to the *Übermensch* appear throughout *Thus Spoke Zarathustra*, and Nietzsche does not mention it by name again until his 'autobiography', *Ecce Homo* (1888), where he writes more about *TSZ* than anything else. Indeed, as we saw in the previous chapter, it is Zarathustra who heralds the coming of the *Übermensch* as the 'meaning of the earth'.

Although Zarathustra admits he is not the *Übermensch*, he is its prophet, and as such seems to understand what the *Übermensch* comprises.[2] The *Übermensch* is a supremely creative type, who embodies the full realization of the overcoming of Christian values. Zarathustra himself stands in opposition to Christianity, but he comes at a time when the dead God still lingers on. The *Übermensch* is thus a vision of humanity that has not yet come into being, a future being who can fully accept God's death and has the capacity to create in the absence of God.

Indeed, the *Übermensch* is defined by his absence of being (which goes some way to explaining why the term necessarily eludes precise definition). *Becoming* and the *overcoming* of human being define the *Übermensch*. Thus, Zarathustra asserts that man is a 'dangerous transition', who moves in his or her overcoming between animal and *Übermensch* (*TSZ*, Prologue 3).

The dynamic movement and fluidity of identity of the *Übermensch* is in strong contrast to the 'last man' (or 'ultimate man') also described by Zarathustra. While the *Übermensch* responds actively to nihilism by creating his or her own values, the last man responds passively by deferring to universal knowledge. The last man advocates the will to truth and dwells in the dispassionate comfort and security of knowledge of things. Nietzsche believed that nineteenth-century Western culture was moving towards the realization of the last man, who represents the (Hegelian) belief that the ideal of life has already been realized through historical progress and the pursuit of reason. The last man is completely happy because he believes he possesses complete self-knowledge and knowledge of everything that has ever happened. Zarathustra rather amusingly tells us that the last men 'blink', which is to say that they suffer a physiological disorder – a neurotic twitch – indicative of their incapacity to see genuine human possibility.

Perhaps the most convincing interpretations of the *Übermensch* are those that define it in terms of a creative process of uniting instincts. In contrast both to the last man, who represses his instincts in order to control them, and to the slave, who has no natural outlet for his or her instincts and is subsequently forced to internalize his or her aggression (as we saw in Chapter 1), the *Übermensch* is able to promote and harness the chaos of his conflicting instincts to his own creative ends. Thus, the Nietzsche scholar Arthur Danto writes:

> The *Übermensch* . . . is not the blond giant dominating his lesser fellows. He is merely a joyous, guiltless, free human being, in possession of instinctual drives . . . and so he is in a position to make something of himself rather than being the product of instinctual discharge and external obstacle.[3]

Of the *Übermensch*, Walter Kaufmann similarly notes that he has 'overcome his animal nature, organized the chaos of his passions, sublimated his impulses, and given style to his character'.[4] Similarly, I have elsewhere interpreted the *Übermensch* as one who is able to coordinate and harness his or her chaotic impulses in accordance with the will to power as the creative law of life.[5]

The *Übermensch* requires immense strength of will to shape and create out of the conflict and strife of life. Indeed, Nietzsche observes that commonplace beings 'perish when the multiplicity of elements and the tension of opposites, i.e. the preconditions for greatness in man, increases' (*WP* 881). The *Übermensch* needs to be physiologically well disposed to be able to endure such inner tension. But such strength is not so much that of the lion as it is the spiritual strength of the child, who playfully recreates itself, unconscious and untroubled by its nature.

The *Übermensch* cannot be pinned down and the content of its nature examined because it is identified with the very process of becoming. The overcoming of instincts is a continual cycle of self-perfecting:

> The man who has overcome his passions has entered into possession of the most fertile ground . . . [T]o *sow* the seeds of good spiritual works in the soil of the subdued passions is then the immediate urgent task. The overcoming itself is only a *means*, not a goal; if it is not so viewed, all kinds of weeds and devilish nonsense will quickly spring up in this rich soil now unoccupied, and soon there will be more rank confusion than ever was before.   (*WS* 53)

Thus, the worst-case scenario for Nietzsche is when the creative process comes to a stand-still, when instincts are satisfied and envisioned goals are realized. This occurs when antithetical forces disengage from each other and lose their mutual tension. In this case, one impulse often comes to dominate the other, rendering their relationship unproductive. A good example of this is the Christian teaching of the victory of good over evil – a situation that Zarathustra seeks to rectify by redressing its unproductive balance through the restoration of creative tension. The *Übermensch* therefore embodies Zarathustra's teaching that 'the highest evil belongs to the highest goodness' (*TSZ*, 'Of self-overcoming'). As Nietzsche says elsewhere,

> One cannot be one without the other . . . [W]ith every growth of man, his other side must grow too . . . That man must grow better *and* more evil is my formula for this inevitability.
>
> (*WP* 881)

And yet this does not mean that the *Übermensch* strives to express all aspects of his personality equally. Indeed, this would entail a particular form of organizational weakness that Nietzsche calls 'decadence'. Decadence is the opposite of creative tension; it is a stagnant composite of unintegrated values, rather than a dynamic and creative whole. The *Übermensch* therefore seeks to bring together his or her contradictory aspects in whatever ratio happens to facilitate the greatest creative tension between them at any given moment.

The *Übermensch* ought not to be regarded as a human being elevated to God-like status, or as a symbol of absolute power. (After all, Zarathustra claims that we desire the *Übermensch* only after the gods are dead.) The *Übermensch* is divine in the sense that it *feels* itself to be divine, and as exuding immense power in its capacity continually to strive and create beyond itself. Such striving inhibits the desire for absolute power. Joy of life is found only in the creating of desire for itself.

When we refer to the natural, creative aspects of the *Übermensch*, we are referring to what Nietzsche calls 'Dionysus' or the 'Dionysian' impulse. For instance, when we say that the *Übermensch* is 'true to the earth' and that it utilizes nature's cyclical power of coming to be and passing away to substantiate its own identity and values, we are effectively saying that the *Übermensch* is a Dionysian man. So what, or who, is Nietzsche's Dionysus?

Dionysus

We have already noted Nietzsche's reverence for the ancient Greek age. For instance, he praises the ancient Greeks for their tragic affirmation of the horrors of life's ceaseless flux, and he found in the Homeric hero's approach to life the epitome of master morality. Now, in the ancient Greek demi-god Dionysus, we find Nietzsche's faith embodied.

Dionysus is Nietzsche's preferred role model for us all. Several times he calls us to invent and create (Greek) gods for ourselves, for 'the invention of gods, heroes, and supermen of all kinds' is the very justification for the 'sovereignty of the individual' (*GS* 143). For instance, Nietzsche's madman, after declaring the death of God, suggests we become gods and invent 'sacred games', such as those of Olympia in Greece. Greek gods are the best role models because they are constructed in 'an ideal image of [our] own existence' (*BT* 3). They are superior to Christ (who instils an inferiority complex in us with his model of perfection (*HAH* 132–3)) because they combine virtue with all too human traits. Humanity and divinity are, thereby, equally exalted (*HAH* 222, 65).

While Greek gods are great role models for us, Dionysus is the greatest of all because he symbolizes the image of a natural and authentic existence, one that heroically affirms the suffering and joy in the continual cyclic struggle of destruction and recreation.

'Have I been understood? – *Dionysus versus the Crucified*' is the final line to his final work, *Ecce Homo* (1888). Dionysus here symbolizes Nietzsche's philosophical project. And in 1889, a year after his mental collapse, we find Nietzsche adopting Dionysus as a personal identity, signing his letters on behalf of the demi-god. We shall soon elaborate on Nietzsche's distinction between Dionysus and the Crucified as two contrasting religious types – a distinction that represents the difference between his own 'religious' project and that of Christianity. Before we do so, let us first turn to the ancient Greek myth of Dionysus to get a sense of who he was.

Dionysus was born of an incestuous coupling between Zeus and his daughter Persephone. In her jealousy, Hera, wife of Zeus, aroused the Titans to attack the infant. These monstrous beings enticed Dionysus with toys and cut him to pieces with knives. After the murder the Titans devoured the dismembered corpse; but the heart of Dionysus was saved and brought to Zeus by Athena. Zeus made mead out of the heart before swallowing it, and gave the mead to Semele – a mortal priestess of Zeus – to drink. Through the coupling of Zeus and Semele Dionysus was born again.

There are several versions of the myth, but a significant aspect that unites them is Dionysus' double birth, first as an immortal and then as a mortal. We must bear in mind, however, that just as Nietzsche reinvented the Persian prophet Zarathustra to serve his own ends, the Greek demi-god Dionysus undergoes a slight revision in his hands. Moreover, the meaning and role of Dionysus changes for Nietzsche in the course of his writing. Thus, in his early writings Nietzsche tends to exaggerate Dionysus' irrational aspects, focusing on his penchant for horror and rapture and passing over his capacity as a mild and gentle ruler. In *BT*, for example, Dionysus represents barbaric, unrestrained passion (as a primitive god of intoxication, wine and music), and he is pitted in exaggerated opposition to the Greek god Apollo, who represents, for Nietzsche, reasoned structure and order (as a god of higher civilization, medicine, healing and law). These gods represent opposing tendencies or impulses in art, humanity and life in general that require each other in our creative endeavours. The Dionysian on its own is dangerous and shatters subjectivity; it needs the containment of the Apollonian. Likewise, the Apollonian achievement cannot be appreciated fully until the Dionysian is acknowledged as its source of nourishment. Crudely put, the Dionysian represents our instincts and Apollo our reason. In Nietzsche's later work, however, Dionysus proffers his own sense of order, as the god there represents 'passion controlled'. It is Nietzsche's later formulation of Dionysus that is strongly opposed to the figure of Christ.

The meaning of Nietzsche's autobiographical statement, *'Dionysus versus the Crucified'*, is fleshed out in a note of 1888 (*WP* 1052) where he discusses the two as distinct religious types.

Their typology is determined by their contrasting approaches to suffering. 'The Crucified' symbolizes final redemption from the human condition, a delusory need for a life without suffering and a resurrection into a better life. Dionysus, by contrast, affirms the suffering of our human life because he is born back into this life (through a mortal mother), despite the immense pain he knows it holds. Nietzsche claims that for the Christian, suffering 'is supposed to be the path to holy existence', whereas Dionysus' understanding of suffering is a 'tragic meaning' where life 'is counted as *holy enough* to justify even a monstrous amount of suffering'. Dionysus does not want to escape suffering, but to affirm it. Suffering in this 'tragic' sense is thus not an objection to life but something to affirm because it is part of life.[6]

In Dionysus we find reason to argue that Nietzsche is not against all religion per se, but against that type of religion that negates life and human experience. Nietzsche has religious faith in Dionysus the noble god, who represents in his cycle of birth, death and rebirth the creative dynamics of life. Indeed, at the end of *Twilight of the Idols* we find Dionysus the subject of the most explicitly religious passages in Nietzsche. Here Nietzsche describes 'the highest of all possible faiths' that he has 'baptized' with the name Dionysus (*TI* 'Expeditions of an untimely man' 49). The Dionysian will is for 'eternal life', and this will is 'experienced religiously' (*TI* 'What I owe to the ancients' 4), for in a Dionysian state one realizes in oneself 'the eternal joy of becoming' (*TI*, 'What I owe to the ancients' 5).

Nietzsche's religious faith is in Dionysus. In a late note of 1888, a faith in Dionysus is described as:

> an urge to unity, a reaching out beyond the personality, the everyday, society, reality, across the abyss of transitoriness: a passionate-painful overflowing into darker, fuller, more floating states; an ecstatic affirmation of the total character of life as that which remains the same, just as powerful, just as blissful, through all change; the great pantheistic sharing of joy and sorrow that sanctifies and calls good even the most terrible

and questionable qualities of life; the eternal will to procreation, to fruitfulness, to recurrence; the feeling of the necessary unity of creation and destruction. (*WP* 1050)

The *Übermensch* is Dionysian in nature. (Unlike the average man of the madman's lamentations, the Dionysian man can actually 'smell the decomposition' of the dead God (*EH*, 'Birth of tragedy' 2–3).) There can be no self-overcoming without struggle, pain and suffering. Self-overcoming is a process without end and without reward. It is a terrifying experience in which the self is lost, only to be found in a new form and then lost again; and this process must be heroically affirmed over and over again. Zarathustra proclaims,

> You must be ready to burn yourself in your own flame: how could you become new, if you had not first become ashes? . . .
> I love him who wants to create beyond himself and thus perishes. (*TSZ*, 'Of the way of the creator')

We need what Nietzsche calls the 'Yes-saying instinct' (the instinct of the child), and it is this that gives Dionysus the strength for *amor fati* (love of fate or necessity), the strength to transmute the horrors of eternal flux into the Dionysian joy (intoxicated bliss, even) of tragic acceptance. Dionysus is Nietzsche's

> ideal of the most exuberant, most living and most world-affirming man, who has not only learned to get on and treat with all that was and is but who wants to have it again *as it was and is* to all eternity. (*BGE* 56)

Dionysus affirms nothing more than what Nietzsche calls 'eternal recurrence' of becoming, which is 'a Dionysian affirmation of the world as it is, without subtraction, exception, or selection – the eternal circulation' (*WP* 536–7).

Eternal recurrence and suffering

Eternal recurrence is the idea (traceable to ancient Egypt and ancient Greece) that we should live in such a way as to wish to live this life over and over for all eternity. Perhaps the most cited reference in Nietzsche's writings to eternal recurrence appears in a passage reminiscent of Matthew's remarks about a thief in the night (Matthew 24.42–51):

> *The heaviest burden* – What if a demon crept after you one day or night in your loneliest solitude and said to you: 'This life, as you live it now and have lived it, you will have to live again and again, times without number; and there will be nothing new in it, but every pain and every joy and every thought and sigh and all the unspeakably small and great in your life must return to you, and everything in the same series and sequence . . . how well disposed towards yourself and towards life would you have to become to have *no greater desire* than for this ultimate eternal sanction and seal? (*GS* 341)

In *EH*, Nietzsche tells us that the idea of eternal recurrence is the basic conception of Zarathustra. The eternal recurrence is regarded by some as a more important and fundamental teaching than the *Übermensch* (though it is appropriate to regard them as interdependent) – as the principal teaching of Zarathustra, and the core of Nietzsche's faith.

In *EH* Nietzsche tells us that the idea of eternal recurrence came to him as a flash of inspiration in August 1881, while walking through the woods beside the lake of Silvaplana near Sils Maria, Switzerland. He immediately jotted the idea down on a piece of paper with the inscription '6,000 feet beyond man and time'. Nietzsche elaborated on his idea in the decade after his initial experience of it, and his remarks have confused Nietzsche commentators ever since.

The eternal recurrence is an enigma. Some believe it to be a cosmological doctrine on the metaphysical workings of reality; and in support of this claim several passages can be cited where Nietzsche seems to be working out the mathematical possibility of eternal recurrence. There are obvious difficulties with this conception, for it places the eternal recurrence at the level of metaphysical truth, which as we have seen is for Nietzsche equivalent to degenerate delusion. Others regard it as an existential test to separate *Übermenschen* from the herd, or as a moral imperative of the *Übermenschen*, thereby revealing exactly what is willed in the will to power.

Each of these interpretations would suit our purpose for expounding Nietzsche's new faith in place of Christianity. What is agreed in each interpretation is the emphasis placed on living in the here and now and the rejection of a transcendent world to relieve our pain. The eternal recurrence is affirmation of life in which moments of suffering are lived over and over again without the hope for redemption from eternal pain. Indeed, eternal recurrence is a radically new morality that paradoxically redeems us from the need for redemption! It shatters and reverses the Christian meaning of eternity, situating the kingdom of 'god' here on earth and transforming 'every "It was" into an "I wanted it thus!"' ('That alone do I call redemption!', exclaims Nietzsche.) In contrast to the Christian message, the eternal recurrence boldly claims that there is no need to repent of one's past and no need for forgiveness of it. We can redeem the past if we totally affirm it and celebrate all it has been. Redemption is thus a matter of will: that is to say, of our capacity to 'will backwards' and affirm all that has come to be. (And here we again come up against the problem posed by the child in Zarathustra's parable 'Of the three metamorphoses', for we are left wondering how the child is able to affirm a past it does not have.)

Eternal affirmation of Christ in all his ugliness

Zarathustra feels the great weight of the eternal recurrence and finds it abhorrent because if all things return eternally, the Christian God and its corrupt and degenerate values will bloom for all eternity as often as they come to die. Thus, while the death of God gave Nietzsche's madman cause for distress (*GS* 125), and Nietzsche (in *GS* 343) '*the reason for our cheerfulness*', the eternal recurrence resurrects God and brings about a corresponding revulsion in Zarathustra. Zarathustra laments,

> Alas, man recurs eternally! The little man recurs eternally! . . .
> [E]ternal recurrence even for the smallest! That was my disgust
> at all existence! Ah, disgust! Disgust! Disgust!
>
> (*TSZ*, 'The convalescent' 2)

The little man who recurs eternally can be interpreted as the
Christian God or man of Christian faith. Nietzsche's faith in
eternal return therefore requires the affirmation even of that
which negates life. In other words, it demands the celebration
of Christ and all that opposes Nietzsche's Dionysian faith. In a
passage entitled 'For the new year', we discover what may be
Nietzsche's eternal new year's resolution:

> *Amor fati*: let that be my love henceforth! I do not want to wage
> war against what is ugly. I do not want to accuse; I do not even
> want to accuse those who accuse. *Looking away* shall be my
> only negation . . . some day I wish to be only a Yes-sayer.
>
> (*GS* 276)

Just as Zarathustra was admired by the ugliest man for turning his head away in shame at the sight of the man's ugliness,
Nietzsche hopes for the time when he too can affirm the
ugliness of Christianity, rather than attack it with his philosophical hammer. Judging from the writing that followed *GS*,
Nietzsche was unable to realize his new year's resolution, for
it is saturated with accusation and *ressentiment*. Indeed, *TSZ* –
the work Nietzsche wrote next, which is, he claims, primarily
concerned with eternal recurrence – is brimming with melancholy and, arguably, affirms very little. However, as the Nietzsche
scholar Bruce Ellis Benson notes, it is perhaps only in his
madness that Nietzsche is able to affirm life and escape *ressentiment*, and thus become a true disciple of Dionysus. For in
his chaotic, irrational state (a state associated with Dionysus)
Nietzsche identified with Christ, signed his letters as 'the
Crucified' and claimed in one 'I have also hung on the cross'
(letter to Cosima Wagner, 1889). In this respect, Nietzsche could
be regarded as having utilized the yes-saying instinct, and as
having affirmed that which he deems most ugly. Nietzsche
remains true to his faith (of affirming life to its fullest), and he

could only do so by giving himself completely to Dionysus and living his life in madness.[7]

Higher men and free spirits

It is not uncommon for people with a passing familiarity with Nietzsche's work to conflate the notions of *Übermensch*, higher man and free spirit. And it is easy to get confused when we consider that Nietzsche only briefly alludes to his various conceptions of human possibility, and that these conceptions are multiplied further in the different translations of his texts. For instance, out of context the term 'higher man' could be construed as Nietzsche's name for a type that is antithetical to the commonplace man or woman of the herd. It is then a short step to identifying this higher man with the *Übermensch*. And yet, as we shall soon see, the higher man cannot surpass himself and thus aspire to *Übermenschlichkeit*. Similarly, the 'free spirit' could be interpreted as a person who, like the *Übermensch*, is not constrained by the moral values and traditions of the herd. Although this is an appropriate understanding, in some instances, of the free spirit, it is not the case in others; for as we shall see, 'free spirit' covers several stages in the development of a person, which evolve from the constraints of herd-thinking to the maturity of *Übermenschlichkeit*.

Generally speaking, the higher man and free spirit are similar in their capacity to respond actively to nihilism. They are spiritually stronger than commonplace men or women as they have the spiritual strength to carve out their own individual, creative niche and develop as individuals. However, in the case of the higher man, and in some instances of the free spirit, they are somewhat limited in their capacity to create beyond themselves and to experience their creations with joy.

The higher man is no more able to overcome himself than the 'last man'. Unlike the last man, however, the higher man cannot tolerate the meaninglessness in the wake of the death of God, and he suffers from it. The higher man is compelled to find a reason for his suffering existence. He is a tormented romantic, who expresses his struggle against social convention through his art; and he turns to his work as justification for his life. Higher men are, Nietzsche says, 'fanatics of *expression* "at any cost"', finding new and more profound ways to communicate their sense of being. They are:

> great discoverers in the realm of the sublime, also of the ugly and horrible, even greater discoverers in effects, in display, in the art of the shop window, one and all talents far beyond their genius – virtuosos through and through, with uncanny access to everything that seduces, lures, constrains, overwhelms, born enemies of logic and straight lines, constantly hankering after the strange, the exotic, the crooked, the self-contradictory.
>
> (*BGE* 256)

Although Nietzsche says that the higher men have talents beyond their genius, he also claims that their aspiration outweighs their creative achievement, causing them to fall from their height. In other words, their creative drive inevitably dries up and can no longer sustain the power of their previous creations. Nietzsche tells us there will come a time in the life of the higher man when he finds his work no longer justifies his existence. At this point he will tire of his creation and struggle to express himself accordingly. When this happens, the higher man cuts his losses and returns to the comfort of the Christian approach to life. The higher men 'collapse and sink before the Christian Cross' because they are not 'profound or primary enough for a philosophy of *anti-Christ*' (*BGE* 256).

In the *BGE* passage above, Nietzsche alludes to Napoleon, Goethe, Beethoven, Stendhal, Heinrich Heine, Schopenhauer and Richard Wagner as higher men. Although these figures were considered representatives of the ideal values of 'the fatherland', Nietzsche tells us they became so only when they were 'taking a rest from themselves'.

It is important to note that although eight 'higher men' make an appearance in *TSZ* Part Four (the book that immediately precedes *BGE*), Nietzschean scholars disagree as to whether these characters are intended by Nietzsche to be of the same kind as we find in his more general discussions. The eight 'higher men' whom Zarathustra encounters on his wanderings are a soothsayer, two kings, a bleeding man (or 'the leech-man' or 'the conscientious in spirit'), a magician, the last pope (whom we met in our previous discussion on pity and the death of the God of compassion), the ugliest man (whom we were introduced to as the murderer of God), a voluntary beggar (or 'sermonizer on the mount') and the shadow.[8] Zarathustra meets these figures on separate occasions and invites them to his cave for a 'last supper' as part of a blasphemous festival during which the higher men worship an ass as God.

Unlike the higher men of Nietzsche's general discussion, the higher men of *TSZ* do not return to Christianity, but turn to Zarathustra for guidance in their suffering. In this respect they are similarly incapable of self-overcoming, and therefore cannot be regarded as Zarathustra's true disciples (for discipleship in Nietzsche's faith requires one to guide oneself).[9] Of these higher men Zarathustra laments: 'The worst about you is: none of you has learned to dance as a man ought to dance – to dance beyond yourselves! What does it matter that you are failures!' (*TSZ*, 'Of the higher man' 20). While Zarathustra is disheartened by the ultimate failure of the higher man's inability to surpass himself, the free spirit, by contrast, is celebrated by Nietzsche simply in its attempt to overcome itself, irrespective of whether it succeeds.

Free spirit

Nietzsche's concept of 'free spirit' can be confusing, for not only does he differentiate his understanding of the term from his contemporaries' supposed misunderstanding of it, but he also alludes to different stages within the development of the free spirit itself, so that the early stages (of immature 'free-spiritedness') barely resemble his ideal (of the fully realized 'free spirit'). Let us try to clarify these different connotations of the free spirit.

According to Nietzsche, the fraudulent so-called 'free spirits' of his time were anti-authoritarian social reformers devoted to democratic ideals. Although these alleged free spirits were courageous enough to challenge authority, Nietzsche considered them to be fundamentally constrained by the prevailing values of their day (notably the herd and slavish ideals of pity, security, comfort and an easier life for all). For instance, although Nietzsche approved of David Strauss' attempt to de-deify Christ in his work *Life of Jesus* (1835), he does not think Strauss has made a sufficient break with those Christian values instilled in him since childhood, which continue to inform (or infect) his work. Nietzsche's notion of 'free spirit', by contrast, promotes experimentation beyond contemporary values, in order to take on a variety of perspectives that enhance its growth and feeling of power.

In Chapter 1 we described the will to power as the capacity to 'stomach' life, and in *BGE* Nietzsche tells us ' "the spirit" is more like a stomach than anything else'. This is because the spirit digests or binds together contrary perspectives and is aware of those unsavoury outside influences that would – to continue the analogy – cause indigestion. Free spirits are thus persons who can determine what, how and when to assimilate experiences from life. They are free from the dictates of tradition, sources of authority and the monotony of habit, and thus free simply to 'taste' life and experiment with it. Free spirits adopt only fleeting habits that enable them to view things from several perspectives. This is important, for it allows them to change their opinions with relative ease and also prevents them from becoming attached to anything (whether it be their 'dearest friend and most glorious human being', those values they most admire in themselves or even the spirit of detachment itself), for attachment inadvertently establishes habit, ideals or traditions.

Because the free spirit cultivates a sense of self-sufficiency independent of tradition, he or she must tolerate immense isolation from others. Nietzsche says that free spirits have to be immoral traitors in order to advance, which explains both why free spirits are often feared and hated by those around them, and why they often find relationships with others stifling.

Free spirits are in themselves experimenters in self-advancement, but their capacity to achieve this depends strongly on the developmental stage of 'free-spiritedness' they have reached. In his 1886 preface to *HAH*, Nietzsche describes these stages in relative detail. Before describing these stages, it is important to note that the free spirit does not possess free will. Nietzsche believes that free will is an illusion. Our will is determined by our physiology, which means that freedom is an expression of health or strength of will, and free spirit is, likewise, a manifestation of 'great health'. Thus, progression through these stages is not a matter of choice or conscious volition; it is, rather, an inner vocation that commands us, or a 'necessary task' that 'wants to become incarnate and "come into the world"'.

According to Nietzsche, the 'ripe' and mature free spirit lies dormant 'like an unconscious pregnancy' within a person, who at the beginning of its development is totally unaware of its intentions. Indeed, this person endures life as a fettered spirit (which is a stage equivalent to the burdened camel of Zarathustra's parable of the three metamorphoses). While the majority of people remain at this stage, the enlightened few will experience what Nietzsche calls a 'great liberation'. This entails one instinct or impulse taking command and mastering the whole soul, estranging it from all it had hitherto revered and loved. The person experiences this sudden release from the fetters of contemporary herd-values as a dizzying sickness, which has the potential to destroy its victim. If the person can tolerate such disorientation, he or she will find himself or herself driven – by sheer wilfulness and temptation – both to destroy and reverse those values he or she previously endorsed. And in order to succeed in this, the person requires a 'morbid' and 'suffocating' solitude. (In terms of Zarathustra's parable, the spirit here is like the warrior lion.) After this excruciating time, the person will experience exuberance and subtle happiness: a stage Nietzsche calls 'birdlike freedom', where the person enjoys life from a wider range of perspectives, before he or she is drawn again closer to life, to feeling and feeling for others. Nietzsche describes this as an 'opening of the eyes to what is close at hand' (which is in contradistinction to the 'last men' who, as we saw above, on p. 60, simply blink and concern themselves with full knowledge of historical events). The free spirit is close to maturity, and must question why he or she needed to experience such isolation and relinquish all that he or she once revered. In asking this, the person comes to the realization that it was done in order that he or she might find the potential space in which to cultivate his or her self-mastery (to become master of his or her values, rather than revering them as having authority and mastery over him or her), to foster greater depth and perspective of life and to experiment with contradictory modes of thought.

Jesus

It is appropriate to outline Nietzsche's reception of Jesus at the end of this chapter, principally in order that we may attempt to contrast his admiration for Jesus with his faith in human possibility and self-overcoming. Needless to say, Nietzsche's reception of Jesus is ambiguous and not as positive as many commentators would have one think. His most developed musings on Jesus appear in *AC*, and take the form of a quasi psycho-physiological profile of Jesus' personality, portraying him as a naïve and sensitive figure to the point of psychopathology. Before this, his scattered comments depict Jesus as a character of warmth, always in contradistinction to the bitter *ressentiment* of the Jewish culture of Jesus' time.

Certainly Nietzsche's admiration did not warrant Jesus being compared to the *Übermensch*. However, there is reason to consider him an immature free spirit or higher man. Indeed, Nietzsche actually describes Jesus as a 'free spirit' (*AC*

32), and it is generally assumed that one of the eight higher men of *TSZ* – the voluntary beggar (also called the 'sermonizer on the mount') – is meant to represent Jesus.

In Chapter 1, we saw Nietzsche keen to oppose Jesus (as an affirmer of life without prescription) to the Pauline Christ (a theoretical invention to enslave life unto death).[10] Throughout his writing, Nietzsche is eager to separate Jesus from Christianity by proclaiming their contradiction. For instance, he asks, 'What did Christ *deny*?' and answers, 'Everything that is today called Christian' (*WP* 158). He is also keen to argue that 'the Church' was constructed 'out of the antithesis to the gospel', so that:

> Mankind lies on its knees before the opposite of that which was the origin, the meaning, the *right* of the evangel; in the concept of 'church' it has pronounced holy precisely what the 'bringer of glad tidings' felt to be *beneath* and *behind* himself.
>
> (*AC* 36)

By placing Jesus outside and at odds with Christianity, Nietzsche grants Jesus free spirit status. Thus,

> [H]e cares nothing for what is fixed: the word *killeth*, everything fixed *killeth*. The concept, the *experience* of 'life' in the only form he knows it is opposed to any kind of word, formula, law, faith, dogma . . . the whole of reality, the whole of nature, language itself, possesses for him merely the value of a sign, a metaphor . . . such a symbolist *par excellence* stands outside of all religion. (*AC* 29)

Nietzsche honours Jesus because he believes that Jesus is not only without *ressentiment* (because he stands outside established values of tradition, and 'has not so much as heard of *culture*, he does not need to fight against it'), but that he sought to eradicate *ressentiment* (by attacking the Jewish Church as a corrupt and self-serving organization). Jesus is an unfettered spirit, and as such he is unconstrained by the unnecessary laws of human dictate and remains 'true to the earth'. The figure of Jesus expresses many traits of the free spirit described above, not least the sense of detached 'bird-like freedom'. Nietzsche claims that Jesus possesses 'the deep *instinct* for the way one must live in order to feel oneself in heaven, to feel oneself "eternal" ' (*AC* 33). Nietzsche revered Jesus for his joyful affirmation of life, and in Jesus Nietzsche saw his own 'glad tidings' pronounced – of a kingdom of God found within one's own heart, free from laws and dogma. Thus, Nietzsche claims, 'True life, eternal life is found – it is not promised, it is here, it is *within you*: as a life lived in love, in love without deduction or exclusion, without distance' (*AC* 29). Also, 'Blessedness is not promised, it is not tied to any conditions: it is the *only* reality – the rest is signs for speaking of it' (*AC* 33).

Jesus is not, however, a mature free spirit. Looking at the stages of development above, we might say that Jesus became stuck when he failed to realize the real reason for his isolation and his relinquishment of those Jewish laws endorsed by others around him. Thus, although Jesus comes to experience a 'bird-like freedom' in feeling himself eternal, and is then drawn close to the earth in his feelings for others, it is at this point that Jesus' spiritual development grinds to a halt. Consequently, Jesus' love for life becomes channelled into a fixation on love for others, and an undifferentiated love for *everybody*. Nietzsche criticizes Jesus' incapacity to sustain distance from people and his inability to differentiate between types of people. For Jesus, Nietzsche laments, 'everything is good' and everybody is equal, and this ideology is antithetical to the free spirit. Thus, Nietzsche claims, 'It is *the problem of order of rank* of which we may say that it is *our* problem, we free spirits' (*HAH*, Preface 7). In terms of Nietzsche's metaphor of spirit as stomach, Jesus proves to be weak in spirit, for he is unable to discriminate between the savoury and unsavoury. Indeed, Zarathustra describes the 'voluntary beggar' (that higher man, who is generally thought to represent Jesus) as having a sluggish stomach that 'wants gentler things'.

Although Nietzsche reveres Jesus' lack of *ressentiment*, and subsequently refers to him as the 'noblest human being' (*HAH* 475), he also criticizes him for promoting 'the stupidifying of man' in placing 'himself on the side of the poor in spirit' and, as a consequence, retarding 'the production of the supreme intellect' (*HAH* 235). However, Nietzsche implies that Jesus might well have continued in his development towards a more mature free spirit, thereby renouncing his immature democratic teachings, had he experienced greater isolation and had he not died 'too early'. Zarathustra concedes:

> [T]hat he died too early has since been a fatality for many . . . Had he only remained in the desert and far from the good and just! . . . Believe it, my brothers! He died too early; he himself would have recanted his teachings had he lived to my age! He was noble enough to recant! But he was still immature . . . His heart and the wings of the spirit are still bound and heavy.
>
> (*TSZ*, 'Of voluntary death')

In addition to being a candidate for an immature free spirit, Jesus can be construed, according to Nietzsche's interpretation, as a higher man. For Jesus in Nietzsche's eyes is compelled to live beyond the established Jewish laws of his tradition; and yet he is both unable to sustain his own creative values and is prone to suffering from extreme self-doubt.

As an alleged higher man in *TSZ*, Jesus (the 'voluntary beggar') is depicted as having renounced his teachings in order to live a more comfortable life, free from all that is unsavoury. Upon encountering this character, we first learn that he has recanted his teachings of love for the poor in spirit (which, as we have just seen, was Zarathustra's wish for Jesus); and we later find him eager to give up altogether his ministry and his search for the kingdom of God (in order to worship his new-found idol, Zarathustra).

Zarathustra comes across the 'warm and cheerful' beggar preaching to a herd of cows on a mount. The beggar tells Zarathustra of his anger and disgust at the depravity of the average person, which were so great that he decided to minister instead to cows (with whom he finds great peace and love).[11] The beggar claims, 'It is no longer true that the poor are blessed. The kingdom of heaven, however, is with the cows.' It is only in becoming a cow and chewing the cud (that is to say, by idling the day away and 'abstaining from heavy thoughts') that one can, he says, enter the kingdom of heaven and effectively eliminate melancholy and the great nausea (nihilism). However, upon gazing into Zarathustra's eyes the beggar is astonished to sense that Zarathustra has himself already overcome nausea and that he affirms life as meaningful. The beggar subsequently reacts in the way Nietzsche elsewhere claims higher men do when they are disillusioned by their own creative endeavours: he relinquishes his individual power to an external authority. Thus, the beggar treats Zarathustra as if he were a gift from God and a divine sign that he no longer needs to chew the cud or seek the kingdom of heaven. The beggar wishes to renounce his cows in favour of Zarathustra, whom he finds 'even better' – to which Zarathustra responds by calling him a 'wicked flatterer', and chasing him away with a stick.

In the following and final chapter we shall see how Nietzsche's faith in human overcoming and the revaluation of values, together with his more positive reflections on Jesus' free-spiritedness, inform a constructive critique of Christianity and Christian discipleship.

4

Testing faith: redeeming Christians from themselves

It is a continual temptation for scholars to try to find common ground between competing ideas, and the desire to align Nietzsche's anti-Christian thought with Christianity is no less tempting. However, the plain fact of the matter is that Nietzsche's thought cannot be reconciled with Christianity, because Nietzsche rejects Christ. Nevertheless, this is not to suggest that Nietzsche finds Christianity to be a completely useless approach to life or that he has nothing constructive to say to Christians. On the contrary, Nietzsche acknowledges that Christianity has its useful aspects. And he has extremely helpful things to say to Christians. Moreover, it will be contended here that Nietzsche's target audience is Christian and that his project attempts to provoke Christians into testing the strength of their faith at the same time as it demonstrates how extremely difficult, perhaps impossible, it is to be what he calls a 'most serious Christian'.

Most serious Christians

It may seem odd, given the forcefulness of Nietzsche's attack on Christianity, to think that he could find it useful in any shape or form. But he gives the impression that Christianity, as an approach to life, can enhance the lives of a select minority. (It is crucial to note that in no way does he recommend it to all, as a universal guide for life.)

Nietzsche refers to this select minority as 'the most serious Christians' who, he says, 'have always been well disposed towards me' (*EH* 'Why I am so wise' 7). We may deduce from this comment that Nietzsche deems Christians 'most serious' when they find themselves open to the severest criticism of their faith and the deepest questioning of the foundations of their being.

Just as we described Nietzsche's philosophy as a faith rather than a system of beliefs, the lessons to be learned from Nietzsche are also a matter of faith. In other words, in reading Nietzsche we will not learn *how* to improve our lives but why it is important to question our lives – to realize our prejudices so that we might overcome them. In an ironic twist to his comment above, Nietzsche's writing is particularly well disposed to Christians precisely because its extreme attack on Christianity is an invitation for the Christian to test the 'seriousness' of his or her faith. In Chapter 1 we saw that a characteristic Nietzsche finds noble is the capacity for non-reaction to that which is disagreeable. Thus, if Christians can stomach Nietzsche's criticism without reacting strongly to it (that is without *ressentiment*) and without feeling inclined to find fault in it, then they have earned the right to call themselves 'most serious' Christians.[1]

Nietzsche's writings call upon us to test ourselves in order to ascertain whether the way we fashion our lives enables us to realize our potential, and whether our beliefs are in the service of our lives or dictate our lives to us. One very effective way to carry out this test is to see how well we cope without our beliefs. As we saw in Chapter 2, the starting point of Nietzsche's philosophy is the death of God, and this scenario provides superb test conditions to assess the strength of a Christian's faith. Nietzsche describes the test of Christian faith as '*the needful sacrifice*'. He says in a passage with this title:

> These serious, excellent, upright, deeply sensitive people who are still Christian from the very heart: they owe it to themselves to try for once the experiment of living for some length of time without Christianity; they owe it to *their faith* in this way for once to sojourn 'in the wilderness' – if only to win for themselves the right to a voice on the question whether Christianity is necessary. (*D* 61)

Nietzsche is in effect calling Christians to assess both the value and limits of their faith by sacrificing it in order to see whether it is strong enough to return. Such a sacrifice can occur only in the solitude of wilderness – which is to say, when the person is confronted with the suffering and horror of life.[2] The test is to see whether the person can joyfully affirm his or her suffering as part of a blessed life (and wish its eternal recurrence); or, by contrast, either wish for his or her escape from it (by seeking comfort in a compassionate God), or feel the need to belittle it (by regarding it as a means to a higher end, such as divine retribution). If Christians can endure the former, then they have successfully lived without recourse to their God and can subsequently pass judgement on whether Christianity is necessary for the living of their life.[3] If they still maintain it is indeed necessary, their faith will subsequently be reborn in strengthened form, as a genuine or 'more serious' faith. If it is not strong enough to return, they are released from an unnecessary restraint on the living of their lives. Christianity, for Nietzsche, is a temporal, human construct, like any other value, and as such it must compete against antithetical values to earn its position as a prevailing value. And in Nietzsche's work we find the grounds for this competing antithesis.

Nietzsche does not think there is a Christian who has the spiritual strength to pass his proposed test: 'The men of the future will one day deal this way,' he says; but not yet. In this respect, the 'most serious Christian' is a myth (which substantiates his claim that 'there was only one Christian and he died on the cross'). According to Nietzsche, the Christians of his day held on tightly to their faith as a shield to defend against life; and as a consequence they prevented their faith from working in the service of their lives. By refusing to let go of their faith they refused its growth and passage back to them in vitalized form. Nietzsche maintains that their faith *becomes* significant, and holds value, only after it has been tested. In response to the Christian who refuses to let go of his or her faith in the belief that it already holds significance and therefore does not need to be tested, Nietzsche says,

No, your evidence will be of no weight until you have lived for years on end without Christianity, with an honest, fervent zeal to endure life in the antithesis of Christianity: until you have wandered far, far away from it. Only if you are driven back, not by homesickness but by *judgement* on the basis of a rigorous *comparison*, will your homecoming possess any significance!

(D 61)

Nietzsche's distinction between what we might call the strong-willed, 'most serious' Christian and the weak-willed, lazy Christian finds an interesting parallel in Dietrich Bonhoeffer's distinction between 'costly grace' and 'cheap grace'. According to Bonhoeffer, cheap grace is to respond passively to one's Christian calling in the belief that one is already saved so that there is nothing to do except enjoy the consolations of redemption. It is, Bonhoeffer says, 'the preaching of forgiveness without requiring repentance, baptism without church discipline, communion without confession' and 'grace without discipleship, grace without the cross, and grace without Jesus Christ'.[4] Bonhoeffer, like Nietzsche before him, criticized the organized Church with its systematic doctrines, rituals and formulas for righteousness, and sought a faith grounded in living experience. In his Barcelona address of 1929, he praised Nietzsche's notion of the *Übermensch* for independently confirming 'many traits of the Christian made free, as Paul and Luther know and describe him'. Both Nietzsche and Bonhoeffer seek an active and costly life in which grace or self-overcoming is earned on an individual basis through continual accomplishment. For Nietzsche, the

one who stands divinely apart in the old style – needs one thing above everything else: the *great health* – that one does not merely have but also acquires continually, and must acquire because one gives it up again and again, and must give it up.

(GS 382)

And for Bonhoeffer, 'Costly grace is the gospel which must be *sought* again and again, the gift must be *asked for*, the door at which a man must *knock*.'[5]

83

Nietzsche does not rule out the 'most serious' Christianity as a noble approach to life. He just does not think any of us capable of it. (Which is not to say that he does not wish a Christian would prove him wrong.) Moreover, he does not think the common Christian is actually aware of the significance of the challenge. Part of the problem, we might say, is that the average person who calls himself or herself a Christian is not aware of what 'faith' actually means, comprises or entails. Time and again we hear Nietzsche both denounce Christianity as 'a system of beliefs' and affirm it as 'a way of life', in order to make the legitimate point that Christians have a nasty habit of using Christianity as a crutch and excuse for not taking responsibility for their own lives. It is not enough to express one's allegiance to the Christian faith; one must embody it and continually test one's faith to determine whether it is necessary and genuine, or habitual and idolatrous.

Nietzsche calls Christians into overcoming their need for the delusory 'truth' of Christianity, and to take it up as a living – and excruciatingly difficult – practice. Christians are offending both their faith and their humanity when they approach Christianity through their will to truth, subsequently regarding it as 'the answer' to questions they feebly construct about 'the meaning' of life and how one *ought* to live it. These questions, Nietzsche says, are the product of weakness, and their answers are dangerous delusions that prevent one from living and directing one's own life. Christianity, Nietzsche says, has become 'a gentle *moralism*', grounded in 'benevolence and decency of disposition, and the belief that in the whole universe too benevolence and decency of disposition prevail' (D 92). Life, Nietzsche argues, is not this simple or cheap! Indeed, such an approach to Christianity has, he claims, brought about 'the *euthanasia* of Christianity' (D 92). A genuine faith is one embodied in struggle and hardship, in which questions must be asked but no definitive answer is expected or sought. Such a faith, Nietzsche says, is found in the will to power, where competing approaches to life are harnessed. If one advocates the will to power and subsequently finds Christianity useful for the affirmation of one's life, then so be it.[6] It is after all, Nietzsche claims, simply a matter of time until a different, competing perspective will overcome the current one, thereby replacing 'Christianity' as the prevailing disposition. Christian faith is justifiable, in Nietzsche's terms, if and only if it is judged as fundamental to one's creative becoming.[7]

Nietzsche the non-conformist

The thoughts of Nietzsche and Christianity should not be regarded as total opposites, rather as competing perspectives on life. We may find aspects of both useful in the living of our own lives, and in this respect reconciliation between these competing approaches can be found on a subjective basis. However, some Nietzschean scholars believe that they have found in his work particular Christian concerns that explain definitively his overall project, thereby reconciling Christian and Nietzschean thought on an objective basis. For instance, Giles Fraser understands Nietzsche's project as a quest for an authentic soteriology, Bruce Ellis Benson explains it in terms of a new pietism and Tyler T. Roberts grounds it within themes of suffering and asceticism. (And we could easily objectify the interpretation in this chapter, calling it something like 'a test of faith' or 'evaluation of self'.) Likewise, scholars have tried to consolidate the link between Nietzsche and Christianity by amalgamating aspects of Nietzsche's thought with the Christian tradition (such as we saw with Altizer's 'death of God' theology), or have attempted to identify parallels between Nietzsche's thought and those of accepted Christian theologians (such as Luther, Karl Barth and Dietrich Bonhoeffer). The drive to unify Nietzsche by relating his thought to other systems of thought – such as Christianity – or by explaining his ideas objectively, can be productive and can add clarity to otherwise obscure notions that we find in his work. However, it is also important to allow Nietzsche's ideas their independence and obscurity, and subsequently to allow our interpretations of his ideas to unravel and dissolve so that others can take their place, or to hold them in creative tension with other, competing interpretations.

Whenever an interpretation of Nietzsche is made (including that in this book), it is clothed in the subjectivity of the interpreter. All scholars of Nietzsche draw out different nuances of his project by bringing themselves into it. The plurality of interpretations and perspectives is true to Nietzsche's project. Paradoxically, we have understood him so long as we do not pin him down and profess a definitive explanation of his thought. Just as Nietzsche claimed Christianity is not a set of beliefs but an approach to life, we can make this claim of his work too. That is to say, instead of taking an intellectual and systematic approach to Nietzsche's work, we can engage with it in such a way as to ascertain whether it is useful for us personally in the affirmation of our own lives. In doing this we apply the message of his teaching to the teaching itself and thereby fulfil its message in the process. Because there is no definitive way to read Nietzsche and no prescribed lessons to learn from him, self-professed atheists and Christians may find aspects of his teaching similarly helpful or unhelpful, depending on how they, as individuals, use it. Nietzsche wants to remove those identity tags and labels we attach to ourselves, and to demolish those boxes and 'pigeon-holes' we place ourselves within, so that we can take account of ourselves in our raw condition as individual human beings.

Nietzsche's argument may well not stand up to intellectual scrutiny. His conceptions of Christ, Jesus, St Paul, the relationship between Christianity and *ressentiment*,[8] to name just four, certainly seem to collapse when carefully examined. But as we saw with his notion of the death of God, Nietzsche's project does not stand or fall according to reasoned argument and the accuracy of his account. Whether you agree with Nietzsche is a matter of 'taste' or, as we described in Chapter 1, your 'physiological disposition'.

Learning from Nietzsche through your response to him

Nietzsche's devastating assault on Christianity is not something either fully to accept or to reject outright. Nietzsche wants to be heard, but he also wants his words to facilitate your own thoughts, rather than dictate to you his own, so that you are free to create in your own image, and not according to his. To this end, Nietzsche would rather you do not agree with him on every occasion (and his provision of contradictory perspectives will prevent you from doing so). Furthermore, he would rather you respond to his writing instinctively and evaluate it according to 'the judgement of your muscles', and not simply absorb it intellectually or scrutinize it rationally.

You learn effectively from Nietzsche when you reflect on your response to him. According to Nietzsche, we attribute meaning to things according to our instinctual relationship to them. By examining our instinctual response to things we can construct an impression of who we are and how we have come to be and, subsequently, how we might become. But what sorts of things might we expect to learn from Nietzsche? How can he make us respond and take account of our own lives and possibly change them?

Unfortunately, as Nietzsche claims, we cannot choose to change our instinctual disposition or the content of our will and our beliefs. Our path to self-overcoming is not a matter of conscious volition and is not something Nietzsche, or anybody, can teach. However, we can still do something to make ourselves more receptive to its possibility, and in Nietzsche's writing we find several suggestions to this effect. Thus, although he cannot give us step-by-step instructions for our individual development, Nietzsche proposes ways in which we can lessen the effect of those aspects of ourselves that inhibit our creative development.

As we saw in Chapters 1 and 3, creative development, for Nietzsche, is a matter of harnessing the tension between opposing perspectives (which is the underlying dynamic of the will to power and of the *Übermensch*). Therefore, if we find we are drawn particularly to one perspective or way of thinking to the detriment of another, we are in a position to try to redress the balance and enhance its creative momentum. To put it another way, if we reflect upon our responses to life and find we have been adopting prejudicial views, we can attempt to determine why we hold them, and in the process reduce our resistance to other points of view. This, of course, is not easy or straightforward in practice. Yet this is what Nietzsche is after. He seeks a life of affirmation free from *ressentiment* (free from the degenerate need to turn the undesired other into a scapegoat for one's own weakness).

Nietzsche believes we can reduce those aspects that limit our creative possibility by affirming *all* aspects of ourselves, and this means exaggerating those aspects that tend to shrink away, and lessening those that are grandiose and overpowering (but not so as to aim for static equality between them). In other words, he suggests that we cultivate tension within ourselves, so that no prejudice or one-sided approach to life can take root. Part of the difficulty of doing this is that it is all too easy to misconstrue which aspects of the self stand in the way of its development. That is to say, it often feels both natural to follow and consolidate one's prejudiced inclinations, and counter-intuitive to want to assimilate that which is undesirable. Yet as we shall see, if we are to overcome ourselves and realize personal growth we need to affirm and rejoice in our undesirable aspects, such as our ugliness and our capacity to suffer.

Know thyself

Nietzsche suggests that we can make ourselves more receptive to the possibility of our self-overcoming by having greater awareness of ourselves and of the extent to which our beliefs dictate and impinge on our lives. In particular, he wants to highlight the dangers of a tendency he saw in Christians to opt for an easy life without struggle. Although Nietzsche regarded this a tendency of nineteenth-century German Christian society, where the social expectation was simply to attend church as a matter of course, in the belief that one's sins were already forgiven, it is also a useful wake-up call for lazy Christians today.

Nietzsche thinks Christians are not only deluding themselves into thinking that life is simply a waiting room for a free ticket away from suffering, they are also offending humanity in the process. Our human life, Nietzsche says, is something to celebrate and own, and this includes its every struggle and pain. Nietzsche calls us out of the waiting room and 'into the wilderness' to confront our suffering and, as we saw earlier, to test ourselves and to force us into learning how to become spiritually stronger and self-sufficient. The Christian who fails to take responsibility for his or her suffering is weak and a slave to suffering. Such a person will not only live a sick and stagnant life but will also create great injustice in other people's lives through their resultant *ressentiment*. Nietzsche illustrates the extent of the negative influence of the 'lazy Christian' and his or her deluded belief that life is a waiting room, in his depiction of the lazy Christian's historical forerunner: the Jewish slave and slave morality.

In Chapter 1 we saw that for Nietzsche the slave epitomizes the person who resents and seeks to overthrow those who are able to take responsibility for their suffering (they are thus just as much slaves to themselves as they are to their masters). And Nietzsche was alarmed that the historic revolt of the exiled Jews had managed to undermine the creative potential of modern society, causing its degeneration. Not only did it lead to the suppression of the spirit of humankind, but there is a sense, in Nietzsche's depiction, in which it led to the suppression of God also. Thus, Alistair Kee suggests that when Nietzsche complains about what is happening to the noble men in the midst of slavish degeneration, he is also complaining about what is happening to God. Just as Nietzsche talks about slave morality and master morality, Kee claims that Nietzsche implicitly refers to two types of God: a 'higher God' and a 'degenerate

God'. The pre-Exilic Jews worshipped the 'higher god', who took pleasure in creating the natural world and who looked upon his handiwork and 'saw that it was good', before turning to his greatest creation: man made in his own image. By contrast, the post-Exilic Jews and Christian traditions have rejected the natural and created a degenerate god in their own image: a projected image of their *ressentiment*.

What, then, can we personally learn from this slave revolt? The answer lies in Nietzsche's insistence that we realize the dangers of projecting disowned aspects of our selves (both good and bad) into our conceptions of God and on to other people. If we are able to accept our weaknesses, failures and limitations we are less likely to react to them and to seek an illusory external source for them – a scapegoat – that we subsequently blame for our failings and seek to destroy with our revenge. If we cannot accept our misgivings, the God we seek is an illusory one: a phantom of ourselves that seeks only to punish our perceived enemies (which are those aspects of ourselves we cannot yet own). To accept our misgivings is to relate to God in a healthy way: enabling us to live, create and grow authentically. In this sense Nietzsche wants us to scrutinize our motives in order to prevent us from deluding ourselves and wrongly accusing and harming others.

And we must question our motives at all times, even on those occasions when we perceive ourselves as living nobly. Thus, we learn from Nietzsche that pity – a feeling that we might ordinarily regard as positive and honourable – can actually alienate and intensify the suffering of the person pitied. You must ask yourself why your pity compels you to help a person you perceive to be in need. For instance, is there a possibility that you do so in order to feel good about yourself? Does it bring you advantages? Does it make you feel superior?

Nietzsche contends that you must first love yourself before you can love another. If you cannot do so, the tendency to split off parts of yourself and project them on to others proliferates. However, Nietzsche requires us also to maintain a sense of distance from ourselves (which is why Zarathustra celebrates those who 'despise' themselves) so that we continue to desire our self-overcoming.

An important part of this realization is learning to love ourselves and accepting our lot in life – not in order that we can settle for who we are but so that we can become autonomous and no longer seek ourselves in others. Such autonomy does not mean we are free to become whatever we desire; it means, rather, that in addition to affirming our aspirations we affirm our limitations and do not perceive them as a lack or cause for suffering. Of course, such ideas are not unfamiliar to the Christian tradition, which affirms humanity as the image of God. But Nietzsche is desperate for us to be able to embrace humanity in its own right, without recourse to or comparison with anything else.

Nietzsche teaches us to embrace and rejoice in those aspects of ourselves that we ordinarily attempt to detach ourselves from: our 'ugliest' side (whether it be a character trait, such as pity; something we have done, such as the notorious murder of God; or that which we most detest and resent in others, such as Christ for Nietzsche himself). Nietzsche wants us to approach our most humiliating aspects as if they were divine or blessed, and to be innocently unaware of their difficult connotations – as a child would be. Although Nietzsche would like us to be able to affirm our ugliest aspects to the extent that we wish for their eternal recurrence, he makes it clear that we are unable to do so. (This is a capacity for the *Übermenschen* of the future.) The best we can hope for is to try to become aware of them and to own them as parts of ourselves. Even this, Nietzsche claims, requires great reserves of spiritual strength that the average person does not have.

Divine risk and experiment

Divinity in Nietzsche is found within the creative endeavour of humanity. It is personified by the god Dionysus; but it is also reflected in the myth of the 'most serious Christian', who is prepared to give up his or her faith in order to ascertain its worth.

Relationship with the divine is agonizingly difficult to sustain, if not impossible. It requires honesty, continual self-criticism and the relinquishment of personal desires and prejudices to the chaotic flux of competing perspectives. Nietzsche's Zarathustra suggests that we ought to give up our petty rational ego, with its delusions of autonomy and 'proud leapings', and enlist what he calls our higher 'Self' or the 'unknown sage', which 'always listens and seeks' in order to create beyond itself. Zarathustra describes the Self as our whole body – the totality of our instincts. But to give up the ego is too great a spiritual demand for most of us. It is equivalent to the proud lion of Zarathustra's parable of the three metamorphoses, who must abandon his warrior-like will of domination and find the innocent 'yes-saying' will of the child.

To approach the divine, for Nietzsche, is to lose oneself and find oneself reborn (or to find oneself a free and unfettered spirit). Just as Dionysus creates out of destruction, you will find that it is only by losing yourself and those values you rigidly hold on to that you can then re-find yourself and regroup as a spiritually stronger person. Through Nietzsche we learn what it means to become a daring experimenter and 'risk taker', to will the loss of the very structures that purport to give absolute meaning and reason itself. To take on Nietzsche's test is to 'find chaos within oneself' and teeter on the edge of madness. It is a

> temporary self-oblivion . . . that will often appear *inhuman* – for example, when it confronts all earthly seriousness . . . in spite of this, it is perhaps only with him that *great seriousness* really begins . . . that the destiny of the soul changes.   (*GS* 382)

In this respect, Nietzsche's teaching finds a parallel with Søren Kierkegaard's notion of the 'religious' approach to life. The philosopher and theologian Kierkegaard maintained that the religious life is one in which everything is risked, including the capacity for rational thought. The religious life is therefore 'madness' from the perspective of reason.[9] According to Kierkegaard, to be religious is to take continual 'leaps to faith' and to venture to believe beyond understanding. Both Nietzsche and Kierkegaard maintain that we should give up rational structures of meaning as the dictates of life and put our trust in non-rational, instinctual sources of life. Although they differ on what these sources comprise (for Kierkegaard it is the will of the Christian God, for Nietzsche, it is the will of life itself – the will to power), they speak in similar terms of a natural inclination that propels us into taking this leap. Thus, Kierkegaard's description of a 'passionate', 'enthusiastic' and 'eager outreaching' is Dionysian in tone.

Although the divine seems out of reach in Nietzsche's understanding (since his idea of faith requires too great a spiritual strength for us to sustain), we glimpse it in the natural dynamics of life itself, of which we are all part. Nietzsche's faith is of recognizing and affirming who we are, and treating every moment of our lives as if it were blessed.

Notes

Introduction

1 In a draft of a letter to his sister, written in December 1887, Nietzsche writes, '. . . Herr Dr Förster has not yet severed his connection with the anti-Semitic movement . . . Since then I've had difficulty coming up with any of the tenderness and protectiveness I've so long felt toward you . . . Now it has gone so far that I have to defend myself hand and foot against people who confuse me with these anti-Semitic *canaille*; after my own sister, my former sister . . . These accursed anti-Semite deformities shall not sully my ideal!!'

2 It could be argued that Nietzsche's Lutheran upbringing, which was grounded in German pietism, prepared the way for his attack on Christian doctrine in favour of praxis and personal experience.

3 One instance is his choice of rather manic chapter headings in his late autobiographical work: 'Why I am so clever', 'Why I am so wise', 'Why I write such good books'. Other instances are his letters, which include one sent to the King of Italy, whom Nietzsche addresses as 'my dearly beloved son Umberto'; to the papal secretary of state, of whom he requests that His Holiness be told of Nietzsche's veneration for him, and which Nietzsche signs 'The Crucified One'; and another, sent to his good friend Overbeck and his wife, in which Nietzsche writes, 'Right now I am having all the anti-Semites shot' and which he signs 'Dionysos'.

1 Antichrist versus anti-life

1 Scholars have applied this very criticism to Nietzsche's own work, accusing Nietzsche of advocating metaphysical truth in his very denial of it (we shall return to this very briefly when we allude to Heidegger's reading of Nietzsche in Chapter 2). Thus, some scholars maintain that Nietzsche's conception of life as chaotic flux is no less a description of the way life *really* is in itself, than the metaphysical conception of order it opposes. However, others have sought to rescue Nietzsche from this apparent paradox by

claiming that he professes a different notion of truth from the correspondence theory presupposed by this criticism – so that truth for Nietzsche is not a question of correspondence between a belief or statement and an actual state of affairs, but is, for example, grounded in its pragmatic worth or utility for life. The truth-claims of Nietzsche's philosophy are not easily categorized and continue to provoke disagreement among philosophers today.

2 Giles Fraser, *Redeeming Nietzsche: On the Piety of Unbelief* (London and New York: Routledge, 2002).

3 Jacob Taubes, *The Political Theology of Paul*, trans. Dana Hollander (Stanford CA: Stanford University Press, 2004), p. 26.

2 The death of God

1 Walter Kaufmann's translation of *GS*, 1974, p. 279, n. 3.

2 Giles Fraser, *Redeeming Nietzsche: On the Piety of Unbelief* (London and New York: Routledge, 2002), p. 15.

3 Martin Heidegger, 'The Word of Nietzsche: God is Dead', in *The Question Concerning Technology and Other Essays*, trans. William Lovitt (New York: Harper & Row, 1977), p. 61.

4 Eberhard Jüngel, *God as Mystery of the World: On the Foundation of the Theology of the Crucified One in the Dispute between Theism and Atheism* (London and New York: T&T Clark, 1983).

5 Thomas J. J. Altizer, *The Gospel of Christian Atheism* (London: Collins, 1967).

3 Nietzsche's faith: the revaluation of values

1 Chapter 4 proposes an answer in terms of the relinquishment of the ego (which is itself leonine in nature). This may lead one to engage with what Zarathustra calls 'the Self' – a higher 'sage' that embodies a more profound wisdom and greater capacity for reasoning.

2 We could think of Zarathustra as being at the spiritual level of the lion. (We are told in *TSZ* that his shame prevents his trans-formation into a child.) He is also a 'convalescent', who no longer perceives a world of absolute truth, but who is not yet ready to embrace the most affirming thought – the eternal recurrence. To Zarathustra, the eternal recurrence is an 'abysmal thought'.

3 Arthur Danto, *Nietzsche as Philosopher* (New York: Macmillan, 1965), p. 199f.

4 Walter Kaufmann, *Nietzsche: Philosopher, Psychologist, Antichrist*, 4th edn (Princeton NJ: Princeton University Press, 1974), p. 316.

5 Lucy Huskinson, *Nietzsche and Jung: The Whole Self in the Union of Opposites* (Hove and New York: Brunner-Routledge, 2004).

6 It could be argued, however, that Nietzsche's Dionysian suffering, as a call for us to embrace suffering as part of life, is not so different from such Christian conceptions as we find in the Theology of the Cross and Simone Weil, among others. And this, therefore, somewhat undermines Nietzsche's accusation that Christianity seeks only to eradicate pain. Thus, in the Theology of the Cross we find emphasis on the God who, out of love for us, immerses himself in our world in order to suffer with us. Here Christ on the Cross does not represent a means to another life free from suffering, but an expression of love for and affirmation of this life of suffering. Likewise, the French theologian Simone Weil calls us 'neither to escape suffering, nor to suffer less, but to remain untainted by suffering'. She asks us even to consider suffering 'a precious gift' equivalent to 'joy'.

7 Furthermore, that the insane Nietzsche signed most of his letters as either 'The Crucified' or 'Dionysus' suggests that he no longer pitted these two symbols in opposition. In his madness (or Dionysian state of affirmation), *Dionysus versus the Crucified* became Dionysus and the Crucified.

8 Some scholars have attempted to identify who or what these higher men represent historically for Nietzsche. A very lucid account is given in Weaver Santaniello's *Zarathustra's Last Supper: Nietzsche's Eight Higher Men* (Hampshire and Burlington: Ashgate, 2005).

9 Arguably, Zarathustra's disciples are his animals – his eagle and serpent, a flock of birds and a mighty lion. Their presence indicates to Zarathustra that his 'children' (those who are spiritually strong) are near.

10 Interestingly, in *AC* 36 Nietzsche claims that one has to be a free spirit in order to comprehend this opposition, which he here describes as an antithesis between the gospel and the Church.

11 The cows may well represent Buddhism (cf. *WP* 342). If so, the voluntary beggar among cows could represent a comparison between Christianity and Buddhism that Nietzsche often makes. Nietzsche regarded both as spiritually weak and nihilistic 'herd' religions that perpetuate mediocrity and increase pity.

4 Testing faith: redeeming Christians from themselves

1 We could differentiate the '*most* serious' Christians from 'serious' ones. While Nietzsche claims the former are well disposed towards him, the latter, he implies, are not, for they are not yet able to accept views contrary to their own, 'For the present [serious Christians] . . . are provoked and grow angry if anyone gives them to understand that what lies beyond their native soil is the whole wide world! That Christianity is, after all, only a little corner!' (*D* 61).

2 We find a similar notion in the thought of Karl Barth, who in his commentary on Romans (1919) writes, 'The mature and well-balanced man, standing firmly with both feet on the earth, who has never been lamed and broken and half blinded by the scandal of his life, is as such the existentially godless man.'

3 We may assume that the person who has successfully affirmed the horror of life, without recourse to his or her Christian faith, will inevitably find Christianity to be unnecessary. (After all he or she has proved he or she can live without it.) However, from a Christian perspective this is not generally assumed. On the contrary, it is commonly believed that genuine faith is substantiated in those moments when God is experienced as absent. St Augustine, for instance, in *Confessions*, book ten, chapter 27, writes: 'Thou wert within me, and I out of myself, where I made search for thee . . . Thou indeed wert with me; but I was not with thee.'

4 Dietrich Bonhoeffer (1937), *The Cost of Discipleship* (SCM-Canterbury Press, 2001), p. 4.

5 Bonhoeffer, *The Cost of Discipleship*, p. 5.

6 Indeed, in the previous chapter we speculated that Nietzsche's acceptance of Christianity was necessary to his own affirmation of life.

7 There is a similarity here with Paul Tillich's definition of faith as 'ultimate concern' (and of 'idolatry', which occurs when one's beliefs are unquestioned and become complacent). Interestingly, Tillich's notion of ultimate concern does not entail faith in Christianity per se. Thus, one person's ultimate concern for life, or for the god Dionysus, may be as valid as another's ultimate concern for the Christian God.

8 See Max Scheler's short and lucid work, *Ressentiment* (1912), which attempts to reconcile Christianity with Nietzsche's ideas of *ressentiment* and the dichotomy between master and slave morality. Scheler argues that Christian love is not motivated by *ressentiment* arising from a weak disposition. On the contrary, it

is grounded in the noble confidence that through loving one becomes more real to oneself and fulfils the creative urge to express the infinite fullness of being. Scheler therefore claims that it is through loving that one feels oneself noble. Furthermore, Scheler asserts, those values that Nietzsche regards as slavish are celebrated by the Christian *not* in order to spite the so-called 'masters', as Nietzsche maintains, but simply because they provide the opportunity for a person to express their love and the fullness of being.

9 Something that is exemplified by Nietzsche's 'madman' proclaiming the death of God to the rational non-believers.

Further reading

Nietzsche's works are traditionally divided into three distinct periods: early (1872–6), middle (1878–82) and late (1885–8). Rather than describe every book of Nietzsche's, this guide will outline those that are most relevant to the themes of Nietzsche we have explored above.

The first period is relatively quiet in terms of Nietzsche's criticism of Christianity, and is concerned rather with art and metaphysics and the need for cultural regeneration and renewal. This period begins with *The Birth of Tragedy*, where Nietzsche introduces Dionysus as a frenzied opponent to the rational Apollo; and it includes the four *Untimely Meditations*, which respectively examine David Strauss, issues concerning the social value of historiography, Arthur Schopenhauer and Richard Wagner as inspirations for new cultural standards.

The middle period includes the books of the 'free spirit', comprising *Human, All Too Human* (in two volumes), *Daybreak* (or *Dawn*) and *The Gay Science* (or *Joyful Wisdom*). Because these works comprise aphorisms they encourage one to dip into them now and then, rather than read them from cover to cover. In this respect they provide an accessible introduction to Nietzsche's thought. These aphoristic works are thoroughly sceptical. In this period Nietzsche is concerned with deconstructing objective values in order to show how they originate in subjective perspective. He thus seeks to undermine morality by exposing its non-moral basis, and to abolish the transcendent, metaphysical world by accounting for its manifestations in finite, phenomenal terms. In *HAH* we find Nietzsche's first major assault on Christianity. This gathers passionate momentum in *D*, where Nietzsche explains Christianity as a metaphysical interpretation of power and describes St Paul as the power-hungry inventor of its doctrines. *GS* continues Nietzsche's attack on Christianity, where Nietzsche's intellectual destruction of meaning (nihilism) culminates in his famous proclamation of the death of God.

Thus Spoke Zarathustra bridges the middle and late periods, and this book begins Nietzsche's resolution of the intellectual crisis he has exposed – through his faith in the 'revaluation of values'. *TSZ* is in four parts (but scholars continue to debate whether the fourth part is an integral component of the work or is, rather, an appendix to it), and is considered by Nietzsche to be the greatest work ever written, comprising 'such an outrageous attack on Christianity' (letter to Overbeck, 1883). Ironically, in 1914 German soldiers apparently went to war carrying copies of *TSZ* and the Bible together. *TSZ* is a parody of the Bible, rich in parable and metaphor, and its central character, Zarathustra, is thought to parallel Jesus. Zarathustra's teaching introduces us to Nietzsche's concepts of the *Übermensch* and eternal recurrence, but their poetic exposition makes them rather difficult to follow. The many metaphorical layers and different nuances to this work mean that even the most experienced reader of *TSZ* may continue to discover new meanings within its narrative each time he or she reads it. In this respect it is not a good book of Nietzsche's to begin with.

The late period includes *Beyond Good and Evil* which, through its aphoristic style, expands some of the themes of *TSZ* and is thought to be a rethinking of *HAH*. *BGE* explores, among other notions, the ideas of master and slave morality and the free spirit in order to attack past philosophers for their blind acceptance of Christian premises in their consideration of morality. *On the Genealogy of Morals* advances the critique of Christianity expounded in *BGE*, and is considered to be the most lucid of Nietzsche's works. It comprises a preface and three interrelated essays, which survey the evolution of moral thinking with a view to undermining the moral prejudices of Christianity. In *GM* Nietzsche discusses notions of *ressentiment*, guilt, bad conscience, asceticism and the origin of punishment; and he offers a particularly scathing critique of the priesthood.

Twilight of the Idols (which plays on Wagner's opera, *The Twilight of the Gods*) elaborates some of the criticisms of Socrates, Plato, Kant and Christianity found in his earlier works. It also criticises German culture and important cultural figures of France, Britain and Italy in order to show how they are representative of cultural decadence. In contrast to these degenerate types he upholds healthier, stronger figures, such as Napoleon, Caesar, Goethe and Dostoyevsky.

Following *TI* is *The Anti-Christ*, an important late work that expresses Nietzsche's disgust at the way noble values in Roman society had been corrupted by the slavish values of Christianity. *AC* describes Christianity as a psychological and physiological disease that originated in the slave revolt of the Exilic Jews. In this context, Nietzsche discusses several themes, people and aspects of Christian culture, such as Jesus, St Paul, the Gospels, priests, martyrs and the crusades, with a view to demonstrating how Christianity is a religion for weak, degenerate people.

Ecce Homo is a useful introductory book to Nietzsche's work as it surveys all of his published works over the previous 16 years. In *EH* Nietzsche reviews his books individually and offers his explanation, with critical remarks, of their philosophical content and descriptions of how his works were inspired. *EH* begins with three astonishing chapter headings: 'Why I am so wise'; 'Why I am so clever'; and 'Why I write such good books'. And it concludes with the chapter, 'Why I am a destiny', in which Nietzsche predicts that his anti-moral philosophy will annihilate the diseased morality that has been corrupting Western culture for the last 2,000 years. Nietzsche ends this, his final book, in the hope that Dionysus – Nietzsche's god of life – would replace Jesus – god of the higher, metaphysical world – as the cultural standard for future generations.

Finally, a word on *The Will to Power*. This work should not be confused with Nietzsche's intended and never-realized 'magnum opus'. (At the end of *GM* Nietzsche announces a new work with this title, but he abandoned his project, and the material he had collated for it was incorporated into *TI* and *AC*.) *WP* is a collection of his notebooks (written between 1883 and 1888), which were assembled after his death by his anti-Semitic sister Elisabeth, his friend Peter Gast and other members of the Nietzsche Archives. This work gives the mistaken impression that the will to power is the central doctrine of his thought.

Works that examine Nietzsche's thought in relation to Christian themes

As argued in the final chapter above, a variety of interpretations of Nietzsche should be sought and read in conjunction with each other as competing, subjective responses to his project. Below are eight books that are useful introductions to his religious thought but that ought not to be taken as definitive explanations of it. (The works of Fraser, Benson, Lippitt and Urpeth, and Roberts are recommended for their lucidity and careful argument.)

Further reading

1 Benson, Bruce Ellis, *Pious Nietzsche: Decadence and Dionysian Faith* (Bloomington IN: Indiana University Press, 2008).

2 Fraser, Giles, *Redeeming Nietzsche: On the Piety of Unbelief* (London and New York: Routledge, 2002).

3 Hovey, Craig, *Nietzsche and Theology* (New York and London: T&T Clark, 2008).

4 Kee, Alistair, *Nietzsche Against the Crucified* (London: SCM Press, 1999).

5 Lippitt, John and Jim Urpeth (eds), *Nietzsche and the Divine* (Manchester: Clinamen Press, 2000).

6 Murphy, Tim, *Nietzsche, Metaphor, Religion* (Albany NY: State University of New York Press, 2001).

7 Roberts, Tyler T., *Contesting Spirit: Nietzsche, Affirmation, Religion* (Princeton NJ: Princeton University Press, 1998).

8 Williams, Stephen N., *The Shadow of the Antichrist: Nietzsche's Critique of Christianity* (Grand Rapids MI: Baker Academic and Milton Keynes: Paternoster, 2006).

Index

affirmation xiv, xviii, 6, 57, 58,
65, 66, 69, 91, 93; of life xiv,
xv, xvii, 1–3, 14, 18, 19, 21, 24,
28, 30, 31, 51, 52, 53, 55, 63,
66, 68, 69, 76, 77, 82, 84, 85,
86, 88, 96, 97
Altizer, Thomas J. J. 43, 85, 95
amor fati 66, 69
anarchy xiv, xvi
Andreas-Salomé, Lou xii, xxi,
43
Antichrist xiii, 1, 2, 71; *see also*
Nietzsche, works of: *The Anti-
Christ*
anti-Semitism xvi, xxi, 94, 101
Apollo, Apollonian 64, 99
Aquinas, Thomas 45
asceticism 85, 100
Ascheim, Stephen E. xvi
atheism xiii, xix, 40, 41, 86
Athena 64
Augustine, St 97
Avesta 46

Babylonian 18
'bad' 14, 19, 23, 46
bad conscience 19, 21–2, 100
Barth, Karl 85, 97
Bataille, Georges xviii
Beethoven, Ludwig van 71
Benson, Bruce Ellis 31, 69, 85,
101, 102
Bonhoeffer, Dietrich 83, 85, 97
Brandes, Georg xii
Buddhism 96
Burkhardt, Jacob xx

Caesar 100
camel 56, 74
Catholic xvi
child 56–7, 61, 66, 68, 91, 95
Christ xiii, 1, 26–8, 30, 31, 38,
43, 44, 56, 63, 64, 68–9, 73, 76,
80, 83, 86, 91, 96
Christianity: corrupt value of xiv,
2, 11, 28, 30, 42, 44, 56, 68;
sickness of xv, 11–13
Christians, 'most serious' xvii, 17,
80–5, 91, 97
compassion 33, 42, 44–6, 47, 48,
49, 54, 82
creation and destruction xiii–xiv,
4, 54, 55, 56, 63, 65, 66, 92
Crucified, the 63, 64–5, 69, 96
crucifixion 25
cruelty 11, 19, 21
crusades 101

Danto, Arthur 60, 95
death 2, 7, 26, 27, 28, 29, 32, 33,
44, 48, 62, 76; of God xiii, xiv,
xvii, 1, 31, 32–54, 55, 59, 63,
66, 68, 70, 81, 86, 91, 98, 99
Death of God movement, the 43
decadence 62, 100
democracy xvi, 16, 73, 78
Dionysian, Dionysus 54, 59,
62–6, 69–70, 91, 93, 94, 96,
97, 99, 101
Dostoyevsky, Fyodor 100

eagle 96
energy 51

Index

Index

master morality xiv, 13–16, 63, 89, 98, 100
master race xvi, 59, 75
meaninglessness 6, 12, 53, 70
metaphysics 33, 34, 35, 36, 37, 39, 41–2, 43, 44, 46, 67, 94, 99, 101
morality 2, 10, 13, 16, 17, 19, 21, 22, 23, 25, 37, 46, 47, 55, 56, 58, 68, 70, 99, 100, 101; *see also* master morality, slave morality
Murphy, Tim 30, 102

Napoleon Bonaparte 71, 100
Nazism xvi, xvii, 1, 59
New Testament 17, 30, 38
Nussbaum, Martha 7
Nietzsche, Elisabeth *see* Förster-Nietzsche, Elisabeth
Nietzsche, Friedrich: ill health of xi, xii, xiv, xviii, xx, xxi, xxii, 69–70; writing style of xiii, xv, 47, 58
Nietzsche, Friedrich, works of xxi, 64, 99; *The Anti-Christ* xii, 17, 44, 75, 96, 100, 101; *Beyond Good and Evil* xii, xv, 71, 73, 100; *The Birth of Tragedy* xi, xx, 64, 99; *Daybreak* xii, xv, 25, 99; *Dionysus Dithyrambs* xii; *Ecce Homo* xii, xiv, xvi, 59, 63, 66, 94, 101; *The Gay Science* xii, 33, 35, 45, 51, 52, 69, 99; *Human All Too Human* xii, xv, xviii, 74, 99, 100; *Nachlass* xvii; *Nietzsche Contra Wagner* xii; *On the Genealogy of Morals* xii, 14, 17, 100, 101; *Thus Spoke Zarathustra* xii, 33, 43, 45, 47, 48, 51, 58, 59, 69, 71–2, 76, 78, 95, 99, 100; *Twilight of*

the Idols xii, 65, 100, 101; *Untimely Meditations* xii, 99; *The Wagner Case* xii; *Wanderer and His Shadow* xii; *The Will to Power* xvii, 101
Nietzsche, Friedrich August xviii
nihilism xiv, xvi, 7, 51, 52, 53, 56, 60, 70, 79, 96, 99; *see also* meaninglessness

Old Testament *see* Torah
Overbeck, Franz xx, xxii, 94, 100

Paul, St 11, 25–31, 45, 76, 83, 86, 99, 101
Persephone 63
perspective xv, xvi, xviii, xxi, 1, 4–5, 8, 42, 58, 73, 75, 85–8, 92, 99
Peter, St 30
philology xi, xix, xx
physiology xv, xviii, xx, 8–11, 60, 61, 74, 86, 100
pity 11, 15, 25, 48, 49–50, 90, 91, 96
Plato, Platonism 7–8, 36, 44, 100
Pope, the last 48–9, 72
postmodernism xiii, xvi, 41
power 11, 12–13, 15, 19, 21, 23, 24, 25, 27, 29, 31, 51, 53, 55, 62, 71, 73, 99
priest xv, 11, 17, 18–19, 24, 28, 100, 101
Protestant xvi, xix
psychoanalysis xviii, 10, 21

redemption 12, 19, 28, 56, 68, 83
Rée, Paul xxi
ressentiment 13, 15, 16, 19, 21, 22, 23–5, 29, 30, 31, 57, 69, 75, 76, 77, 81, 86, 88, 89, 90, 97, 100

105